MILITARY AND POLITICS IN ISRAEL

Nation-Building and Role Expansion

MILITARY AND POLITICS
IN ISRAEL

Nation-Building and Role Expansion

AMOS PERLMUTTER

FRANK CASS & CO. LTD.
1969

First published in 1969 by
FRANK CASS AND COMPANY LIMITED
67 Great Russell Street, London WC1

©1969 Amos Perlmutter

SBN 7146 2392 X

Printed in Great Britain by
Billing & Sons Limited, Guildford and London

To my Mother and Father

CONTENTS

PREFACE

In 1948 the Israeli War of Liberation thrust the army into prominence, and from that time on army leaders have been influential in the governmental and economic élites committed to rapid modernization. The Sinai victory in 1956, and the third military success in Sinai, Jordan, and Syria in 1967, further enhanced Zahal's (Israel Defence Forces) reputation. Although Israel's standing army is no larger than 80,000 men, one-seventh of the country's total Jewish population of about 2·5 million is in the active military reserve. Given these conditions, it is natural to consider what impact the army has had on the political life of Israel. This study has therefore focused on the nature of civil–military relations in Israel, tracing them from the earliest beginnings of the Zionist movement in Palestine up to the present, and demonstrating in the process the persistence of civilian over military authority, notwithstanding Zahal's extraordinary role as an instrument of nation-building.

In this analysis we shall undertake an examination of the following: (1) the function of military structures and the expectations of military élites both before and after the formation of the state of Israel in 1948; (2) Zahal's doctrine of role expansion; (3) the Israeli formula for civil–military relations; and (4) the role the army plays in the determination of defence and foreign policies. We also propose to challenge a number of hypotheses which have been advanced concerning patterns and types of civil–military relations; among these are: (1) Andreski's contention that a high Military Proportion Ratio—"the proportion of militarily utilized individuals in the total population" —enhances the supremacy of the army;[1] (2) Huntington's contention that the combination of a pro-military ideology, high military political power, and high military professionalism produces military political supremacy;[2] and (3) the rigid preconception—advanced by General Von der Goltz—that a "nation-in-arms" enhances militarism.[3]

None of these hypotheses applies to civil–military relations in

Israel, although the types advanced by Huntington and Andreski suggest that Israel should fit the model of civil–military relations in which the military achieves ascendance over the civilian. Zahal has actually played a major role in creating a predominantly civic culture.

The decision concerning the presentation of the analysis in this book was a hard one. Because there is so little material in English on the subject of recent Israeli history, we have combined our analysis with an historical narrative, thus placing the discussion of the Israeli army in the wider context of Israeli society and politics.[4]

Much of this analysis depends upon an interpretation of the circumstances under which the Israeli military structures were formed and eventually consolidated. Israeli society, its political and social structures, can be explained only in terms of a constellation of factors, no single factor by itself explains the creation of a new social system in Israel or the development of its political structures and its army.

Our historical and empirical examination has taken the following independent variables into consideration:

1. *The Organizational Dimension*
   a. The elements of mobilization.
   b. The degree of organizational and political autonomy.
2. *Sources and Procedures of Mobilization*
   a. The sources of recruitment.
   b. The ideological factors contributing to the cohesiveness of the army.
3. *Political Involvement*
   a. The relationship between military structures and politics.
   b. The political ideology and *Weltanschauung* of military structures.
   c. The extent to which these structures have interfered in politics.

For convenience, our study has been divided into two analytical periods:

1. Pre-independence, 1909–1947.
2. Post-independence, transition and consolidation, 1948–present.

The pre-independence era is related to the post-independence era in the sense that in the former organizations were non-complex and in the latter the reverse was true. In pre-independence, military structures were autonomous (or semi-autonomous), while in post-independence the army became subordinate. Organizational autonomy enhances political autonomy and political intervention. Thus, organizational subordination rendered the army non-political and non-interventionist.

In the post-independence era, we examine the procedures whereby the army assumes the role of nation-builder formerly undertaken by voluntary and autonomous organizations. The section on role expansion is short but suggests the problem schematically. Role expansion contributed to the depoliticization of Zahal's officer corps by internalizing some, if not all, of their political demands and expectations.

Internalization through role expansion is one means of guaranteeing the subordination of the military to civilian institutions and structures. An equilibrium between military and civilian functions is also achieved by a conscious merit policy regarding officer recruitment, promotion, and mobility within the army, and by easing the integration of military men into civilian society after retirement. This is buttressed by a doctrine of rapid officer turnover and limited service longevity for the high command, who are absorbed into the reserve system, providing the country with one of the most effective and resilient reserve systems in the world.

A military challenge to civilian practices and procedures (illustrated by the Lavon affair) widens the scope of both and enhances the position of the Ministry of Defence as the arena for arbitration of civil–military conflicts. This, in effect, removes the possibility of a direct intervention by the army in politics and substitutes a system of alliances between the military and society in Israel.

Sources

Our sources fall into three categories: (*a*) friends; (*b*) direct interviews; and (*c*) experts on specific topics.

(a) *Friends*. I am most grateful to Brig.-Gen. Yigal Allon, former Commander of Palmach and now Minister of Labour, for several days of conversation over a period of many years, on the Palmach, his role, and his relations with Sadeh and Ben Gurion; to former Deputy Defence Minister Shimon Peres; Col. Manes Prat, former Director of the Dimona nuclear reactor; Lt.-Col. Pinhas Zusmann (better known as Siko) of the Palmach; Col. Hilled Aldaag, former Chief of the Army Corps of Engineers; the late Maj. Israel Ben-Hashal; the late Col. Shlomo Altun; Brig.-Gen. Ezer Weizmann, former Chief of the Air Force and now Chief of Army Operations; Brig.-Gen. Yoseph Geva, former Commander of the Central Front, now a military attaché in Washington; Brig.-Gen. Aaron Remez, the first Chief of the Air Force and now Ambassador to London; Dr. Col. Moshe Kelman, Palmach Commander (1948).

(b) *Direct Interviews.* The list is too long (over 300) and most officers prefer anonymity. It includes, however, several intelligence officers and members of Brig.-Gen. (then Maj.) Ariel Sharon's Special Unit 101. Interviews were oral and some lasted for several weeks.

(c) 1. *On Lavon.* Pinhas Lavon, Minister of Defence (1953–1955); Shimon Peres, Deputy Minister of Defence (1959–1965); Moshe Lissak, Professor of Sociology, Hebrew University in Jerusalem; and several army officers and Defence Ministry bureaucrats who prefer anonymity, especially army intelligence officers between 1953–1956.

(c) 2. *On Role Expansion.* Col. Mordechai (Morale) Bar-Onn, former Chief Educational Officer; Asher Ben-Yosef, Director Israel air industry; certain administrators of the Dimona nuclear reactor, including the present director.

My special thanks go to the following individuals in Zahal, at Berkeley, and elsewhere for help in making the study of Zahal more meaningful. In Zahal, I especially acknowledge a unique person who brings strength, modesty, and compassion to the cause, Brig.-Gen. Meir Amit, Zahal Chief of Operations in the Sinai Campaign and head of the Mosad. Brig.-Gen. Yehoshafat Harkabi, a soldier and scholar, and former Chief of Army Intelligence (1955–1959); and Lt.-Col. Yitzhak Oron, the brilliant analyst; all have taught me to better understand the real issues underlying the Arab–Israeli conflict and the Israeli position in that bitter conflict. To Dr. Col. Yehudah Wallach, professor of military and Zahal history, the University of Tel-Aviv, for some ideas and more disagreement. Needless to mention that no Zahal officer is responsible for my analysis and interpretations.

In the profession, my thanks go to Professor Seymour Martin Lipset of Harvard, former Director of the Institute of International Studies at Berkeley, who made this study possible by inviting me to join that Institute. To Professor Moshe Lissak without whom much of this study could not have been pursued; to my friend Professor John C. Harsanyi, of Berkeley, for reading, advising, and constant encouragement; to Professor Aaron Wildavsky of the University of California at Berkeley; to Professor Samuel P. Huntington of Harvard for reading the first manuscript and for encouragement; to Eliezer Rosenstein of Berkeley; and to Dr. Charles Hutchinson, of the Air Force Office of Scientific Research, for support and friendship; to the Brookings Institution and Professor H. Field Haviland for a pleasant year which provided me with the opportunity to complete this study. None of the above bear responsibility for my analysis and interpretations.

My appreciation also to Kay Kintner whose editorial assistance and suggestions have been most helpful in the preparation of this manuscript; and to Judy Mitchell for her excellent typing and meticulous page proof.

Last, but not least, to my wife Nina who has withstood the idiosyncracies of a difficult intellectual.

Aware of the limitations imposed by virtue of this topic; the absence of open documents; the secret nature of the material; the political explosiveness of the issues; the demand on the part of those who co-operated for discretion on the part of the author; their demand for anonymity; and my reliance on speculation in several places where neither documentation nor clear evidence could be evinced, I present this study as a preliminary call for others to follow as well as an outline for further research and interpretation for myself and others.

In May 1968, Zahal created a new rank of Tat-Aluf (Brigadier-General), thus elevating the rank of the chief of staff from Major to Lt.-General. Since our reference is mainly with officers whose given ranks were that of the period of May 1968 and also in view of the fact that some reserve officers were elevated and some were not, we shall leave the ranking as before 1968.

Harvard University   Cambridge, Massachusetts
                                              October 1968

NOTES

1. Stanislaw Andrzejewski (now Andreski), *Military Organization and Society* (London: Routledge & Kegan Paul, 1954), pp. 33–34.

2. Samuel P. Huntington, *The Soldier and the State* (New York: Vintage, 1964), p. 97.

3. Gaetano Mosca, in Arthur Livingston (ed.), *The Ruling Class* (New York: McGraw-Hill, 1939), p. 241. See also David Rapoport, "A Comparative Theory of Military and Political Types," in Samuel P. Huntington (ed.), *Changing Patterns of Military Politics* (New York: Free Press, 1962), pp. 85–86.

4. In English the literature on Zahal is scarce. A brief almanac-type description of the Israeli army is Moshe Pearlman's *The Army of Israel* (New York: Philosophical Library, 1950). See also Ben Halpern, "The Role of the Military in Israel," in John J. Johnson (ed.), *The Role of the Military in Underdeveloped Countries* (Princeton: Princeton University Press, 1962), pp. 317–58; and J. C. Hurewitz, "The Role of the Military in Society and Government in Israel," in S. N. Fisher (ed.), *The Military in the Middle East* (Columbus: Ohio State University Press, 1963), pp. 89–104. Amitai Etzioni, "The Israeli Army: The Human Factor," *Jewish Frontier*, XXVI (November 1959), pp. 4–9, concentrates on cohesion within the Israeli army.

Part One

Pre-Independence Defence Units and their
Political Expectations, 1909–1948

CHAPTER I

Forerunners of Haganah, 1897–1924

THE modern army of Israel has its roots in the security structures of the pre-independence pioneer movement of the Jews in Palestine. These defence units were created by the Socialist-Zionists, the most significant, powerful, and mobilizing elements of Jewish colonization. Socialist-Zionism embraced a wide range of men, ideas, and organizations in both the Diaspora and Palestine, but only in Palestine was it forged into a movement of great consequence. There it came to represent the interplay between Socialist ideological commitments and the pragmatic considerations which modified them. The result was the gradual transformation of a colonization effort into a programme for national liberation. The Socialist-Zionist movement became the chief instrument of nation-building; the mobilizer of the pioneer revolution; the creator of a new society; and the founder of the Israeli army.

The pioneer Zionists had a genius for organization which enabled them to develop very elaborate institutional frameworks prior to nationhood. But this organizational talent did not have the same impact on their early attempts to establish structures for self-defence. It was not until 1925 that the Socialist-Zionists in Palestine achieved a satisfactory instrument for national security, the Haganah (Defence), the true forerunner of Zahal.[1]

In the early stages of Zionist colonization in Palestine, two clearly different concepts regarding a military role emerged. For our purposes, we shall classify these as the Professional Type and the Pioneer Type, each of which can be illustrated by the ideas of one man.

The Professional Type, as envisaged by Vladimir Jabotinsky,[2] was to be a national professional army unaligned to any ideology or political party. It was to serve as an ally of the

B

Mandatory in order to help establish the leadership of the Jewish community (Yishuv) in Palestine. As we shall see, when Jabotinsky's ideas were finally realized—by the National Military Organization (NMO or Stern Gang)—they actually achieved the contrary.

By far the favoured concept regarding the military function was the idea of the soldier as a pioneer. This Pioneer Type is largely based on the theories of Yoseph Trumpeldor, as interpreted and put into practice by the Labour Legion. He saw the defence function as that of assuring the survival of the Jewish collectives, and the discipline of a soldier–pioneer life was a way to achieve both national and personal redemption.

Trumpeldor conceived of a political—military partnership in which the political leadership would always predominate. The military cadre was to be imbued with the ideology of the political élite and to function as its organizational weapon. Working together, these two élites were to act as the chief mobilizers of the nation, creating both a new type of society and a new state.

Hashomer

The first Jewish defence forces were organized in the Diaspora in the late nineteenth century by the Poale Zion party, the precursor of Socialist-Zionism, to serve as guard units during the pogroms. The Poale Zion party also sponsored the development of the first self-defence groups in Palestine which were formed in 1905 and later displaced by a self-defence society called Hashomer (The Watchman) which emerged in 1909).

At its conception, Hashomer was not a politically cohesive unit but a loose combination of Zionists from Eastern Europe, the Ukraine, and the Caucasus. It was originally formed by Poale Zion party members and some veterans of the Diaspora units, but was soon joined by left-wing Jewish Russian Marxists, who brought to it the sort of militance that the Iskra group had introduced into the Russian Social Democratic Labour Party. Its function—providing watchmen for Jewish settlements—was limited. What sustained Hashomer, at least to the middle 1920s, was the proximity of its ideological and national commitments to those of other pioneer Socialist groups. It was, in its early days, an alliance of romantic and rather naïve nationalists from the Caucasus, dedicated Social Revolutionaries, and militant Poale Zionists. The latter group envisaged a proletarian élitist revolution, the former the creation of a "tough Jew", the image from which the nationalistic folklore of Israel has sprung.

The revolutionaries of Hashomer were not content to maintain this "heroic" organization simply as a union of valorous watchmen, as they were fully aware of the opportunities open to them for infiltrating "defenceless" social-democratic groups. What they needed to accomplish this objective was a military élite and a socio-economic base to support it.

To this end, one of Hashomer's spokesmen, Mania Vilbashevitz-Schohet, argued that self-realization through settlement and labour, the chief tenet of Socialist-Zionist ideology, could be accomplished in agricultural collectives defended by Hashomer. A collective in Sejera, a Galilee farm, was set up as a model of this new organizational weapon of Socialist-Zionism. In this scheme, Hashomer was to establish the dictatorship of an agrarian proletariat based in fortified collectives and was to serve as the vanguard of the Socialist-Zionist movement.

Working as a semi-conspiratorial nucleus, Hashomer militants infiltrated most Socialist-Zionist organizations in Palestine to intervene and eventually compete with the work and purposes of the Histadrut (the General Federation of Labour in Palestine) and the Hityashvut (the pioneer settlements system). Thus Hashomer's Marxists, under the guise of providing defence, sought to turn the activism of Socialist-Zionism in a left-wing direction.[3]

Hashomer's embryonic ideology and objectives can be seen in its 1912 Proposal on the Protection of the Yishuv:[4] (1) Hashomer will not limit its role to physical protection of the Jewish settlements; it must inculcate into these people the consciousness that they must defend themselves. (2) Hashomer must provide the nucleus for the *widening* of the defensive functions of the Jewish community. (3) Hashomer has to have a monopoly over the defence of the Jewish community of Palestine. (4) Therefore, Hashomer must serve as the professional-conspiratorial armed force of the Yishuv. To accomplish these objectives, Hashomer, acting as a secret society, also established the organizational and procedural paraphernalia for such activity.[5]

By 1919 Hashomer had become a cohesive group of not more than 100 members; it was no longer a federation of watchmen. Its cohesiveness derived from a variety of sources: Socialist doctrines, watchman experience, communal living, nationalist solidarity, and an heroic folklore. What emerged was not a limited watchman society but a socio-political nucleus led by a revolutionary Socialist and nationalist élite which regarded themselves as the élan of Socialist-Zionism.

Hashomer had partial success in infiltrating the Poale Zion party and the Labour Legion, but it failed to penetrate the Histadrut and the United Labour Party. Even though Hashomer rendered essential services for the collectives, the leaders of Socialist-Zionism—and especially the emerging Palestinian leader, David Ben Gurion—did not approve of its aims and methods, and this culminated in Hashomer's open split with Socialist-Zionism in the early 1920s.[6] It was through the Labour Legion that Hashomer's ideology made its contribution to Socialist-Zionist thought and influenced the development of the kibbutz settlement movement.

Jewish Legions

The next effort to form defence units was made by Trumpeldor, a militant Socialist-Zionist radical and veteran of the Russo-Japanese War of 1905. Early in the First World War, Chaim Weizmann, Jabotinsky, and Trumpeldor decided that a Jewish Legion serving with the allies in the Middle East could prove useful in political bargaining with England for the creation of an independent Jewish National Home in Palestine. Jabotinsky and Trumpeldor also felt that the legion's war experience would create a "new Jewish soldier type", a useful instrument in an activist nationalist movement. However, the British command at Cairo did not favour the formation of an independent Jewish Legion, although it did recommend the establishment of a transport unit, the Zion Mule Corps, which was formed in 1915 and put under the command of a British officer, Colonel John Patterson.[7] This was followed by the creation of two new legions, composed of Jewish volunteers from the United States, Great Britain and Palestine.

The Gdudim (Legions) formed the base for a political structure over which several Zionist factions competed as the war drew to a close. Jabotinsky envisioned the Gdudim as the first stage in the development of a Jewish army in Palestine, but Trumpeldor advocated transferring the Gdudim into the political arena of Socialist-Zionist settlement in Palestine.[8] Trumpeldor believed in security and saw self-defence as one important function of the commune, but he wanted to adapt the military spirit of the legions to the values of the pioneers. Not so Jabotinsky, who wanted to utilize this army as an instrument for gaining influence over the Mandatory. At the war's end, however, the legions were dissolved despite Jabotinsky's concerted efforts to maintain them as the army of occupation in Palestine.[9]

By 1920, rising Arab nationalism added impetus to Jewish efforts to create an independent self-defence organization. Though Arab nationalism during this period was primarily anti-Turkish, it was also anti-Zionist.[10] From the beginning of Zionist settlement in Palestine, Palestinian Arab nationalists were firmly opposed to Zionism. A wave of anti-Jewish Arab activity began in northern Galilee late in 1919, when the settlement of Tel-Hai was attacked but successfully defended by Hashomer and the demobilized legions led by Trumpeldor. The Tel-Hai attack was followed by a chain of massacres of Jewish villagers and pioneers in Galilee, culminating in an organized assault on the Jews by the Palestinian mufti al-Hajj Muhammad Amin al-Husayni in Jerusalem in the year 1920. Jabotinsky organized former legionnaires and defended the Jewish community in Jerusalem, for which he was arrested by the British occupation authorities.

These events persuaded the Jewish community in Palestine that the Mandatory was unwilling to interfere in the Arab–Jewish conflict and therefore would not protect them. At this point they recognized that their own military defence efforts would have to be entrusted to a permanent organization.

Labour Legions

At about the same time that the Zionists were searching for some form of defence against Arab attacks, the British were engaged in consolidating their control over the Mandate which they had just inherited from the Ottomans. This has come to be known as the Kevishim (roads) era.[11]

Communications and road-building were the first constructive works undertaken by the occupying forces to facilitate both military and political administration of the area. In the early 1920s, the Mandatory established a Ministry of Public Works. Road-building was one of its tasks and therefore the Ministry advertised for contractors. Private Arab contractors competed with the Jewish labour unions in bidding for these contracts and the unions won out.

Ahdut Ha-Avoda and Hapoel Hatzair (Zionist labour parties) employment offices co-ordinated their activities, and the labour force came from the ranks of the new immigrants. Here, for the first time, the Israel labour movement acted as a contractor. The work was undertaken on a collective basis. The roads were divided into sections and each group of workers was assigned a specific section. They worked together and lived collectively in camps built at the centre of the roads. The Kevishim served as temporary camps in preparation for independent agricultural work. During the road-building period, a new nucleus of pioneers solidified.

The most unique of the collectively organized groups during the Kevishim era was Gdud Ha-Avoda (Labour Legion). Its nucleus came from Hehalutz (a pioneer movement in Russia). Organization of Gdud Ha-Avoda was initiated by Trumpeldor but the first groups were not formally established until the middle of 1920 (half a year after Trumpeldor's death) at a meeting commemorating this beloved leader. Much like Hashomer, Gdud Ha-Avoda was to serve as a base for Zionist pioneer settlement and defence.

The Labour Legion put a premium on two of the principles of Socialist-Zionism, avoda and haganah (work and defence). Although the Labour Legion participated in road-building, railroad work, and mining, it was actually the forerunner of the kibbutz (collective agricultural settlement), for the legion surrounded the roads, railroads, and mines with camps of pioneers, thus merging the Socialist-Zionist slogans "conquest of labour" and "conquest of land".

When a Gdud Ha-Avoda group joined an Ahdut Ha-Avoda

group on the Tiberias–Zemach road, they put their theory into action—they realized Trumpeldor's special project by establishing a Palestine Grand Commune. Gdud Ha-Avoda set its sights on the goal of "conquering" work in the Kevishim by sending its labour platoons to work in the most difficult and dangerous spots. The spirit of the Gdud, the solidarity and self-sacrificing loyalty of its members furnished a new impetus and new enthusiasm to the Socialist-Zionist movement.

The Labour Legion had a special appeal for the *avant garde* leadership of the third major wave of immigration (Aliyah) to Palestine (1919–1925). This group, numbering some 40,000, seized upon the agricultural commune pioneered by the Second Aliyah (1904–1905) and attempted to make it the foundation of Socialist-Zionism. It was the third wave which formalized and institutionalized the kibbutz system so that it eventually became one of the most powerful organizational structures in Palestine.

The Third Aliyah was a consciously organized group of collectively minded people. The Second Aliyah had been the product of the "Great Despair" era, its people at heart still suffered from the memory of the collapse of the 1905 revolution. The people of the Third Aliyah were the products of practical Zionism infused with the optimism of the 1917 revolution. Although initially hopeful and favourably disposed toward the Russian Revolution, these intellectual and radical Jews became disillusioned when they realized that the new Bolshevik state would not tolerate an independent Jewish existence. Their estrangement from Bolshevism made them turn towards Palestine where they hoped to achieve the social and political egality denied them in Russia.

Gdud Ha-Avoda saw itself as the carrier of the Socialist radical revolution as against the corrosive elements of Socialist assimilationism and anti-Zionism. As the Socialist-Zionist movement headed toward consolidation, the more radical elements were purged. Thus the Labour Legion suffered much the same fate as Hashomer when it was dissolved after being taken over by a militant left-wing group, led by Communists, which attempted to control the management of the kibbutzim. Its more constructive and less radical members were absorbed into the Ha-Kibbutz ha-Meuchad (United Kibbutz Movement) where the Gdud found new life. (See Table 1.)

TABLE 1

The Relationships between the Yishuvs Political Parties and Military Structures in Palestine

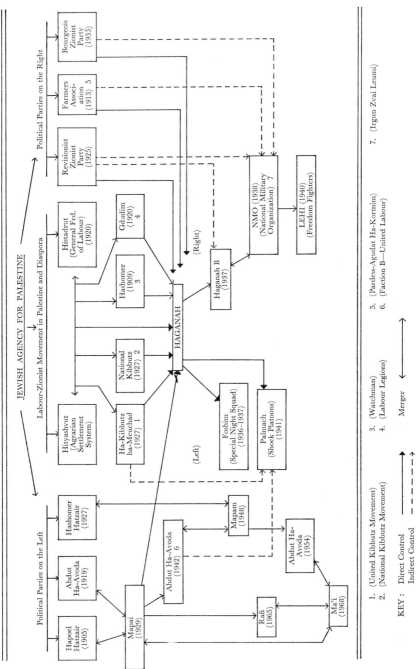

1. (United Kibbutz Movement)
2. (National Kibbutz Movement)

3. (Watchman)
4. (Labour Legions)

5. (Pardess-Agudat Ha-Kormin)
6. (Faction B—United Labour)

7. (Irgun Zvai Leumi)

KEY :   Direct Control   ———→

        Indirect Control   - - - - - →

Merger   ⇒

The Formation of Haganah: The Defence Organization
of the Socialist-Zionist Movement, 1920–1935

Between 1904 and 1920 the organizational basis of the Socialist-Zionist movement was very complex: there were three political parties, three agricultural unions, and three defence societies. Realizing that there was strength in unity, Socialist-Zionist leaders in the early 1920s began to press for the creation of an all-inclusive political party which would integrate all major interest groups. Their efforts culminated in the establishment of Ahdut Ha-Avoda (United Labour Party) in 1919, and Histadrut in 1920.[12] Thus the Socialist-Zionist movement entered a new phase which represented a triumph for Ben Gurion and others who had long striven to make the Labour Party in all respects the party of the nation.

Our movement (Labour) always stood steadfast behind the Socialist ideal which says that the party of the proletariat in contradistinction to the parties of other classes, is not only a party of class, carrying the burden of the welfare of the class, but a national party responsible for the future of the entire nation. It does not consider itself merely a party to the national ideal, but as the nucleus of the future nation.[13]

As early as 1906, when the Poale Zion party was formed in Palestine, David Ben Gurion had advocated the formation of a general confederation of all Socialist-Zionist organizations. Any concerted effort toward unity, however, was hindered by meagre immigration, the First World War, and leftist infiltration. This situation' was reversed in 1920 by large-scale immigration of militant and dedicated pioneers and the concurrent spread of agrarian collective settlements. Also World Zionism began to focus more attention on Palestine and these three factors combined to add impetus to the drive toward consolidation. The final catalyst was the Jewish need for self-defence in face of rising and militant Arab nationalism and the reluctance of the British administration to take measures to curb it. The necessity for creating a central authority to manage the defence of the collectives played a key role in the development of the United Labour Party and Histadrut.

At first, unity and not defence was the objective. Ahdut

Ha-Avoda was conceived as a party of all labour-Zionists: farmers, pioneers, and workers in the settlements and in the towns. Its platform made no provisions for defence, stating as its purpose only "the revival of the Jewish nation; the return of its sons to their homeland, and the resettlement of land".[14] Similarly, the first goal of Histadrut was to pool the human resources of the active Zionist labour organizations in Palestine. With the emergence of the United Labour Party and Histadrut, only the defence societies remained outside their control.

In the collectives, the militants of Hashomer and the Labour Legion had gained exclusive control of the defence function and, as a result, the kibbutzim were relatively secure and well protected. The Jews in the cities were more vulnerable as the Arab riots in Jerusalem and Tel-Aviv clearly demonstrated. Had it not been for the support of the partially demobilized Jewish Legions, the cities would have fallen easy prey to Arab abuse. By contrast, the agrarian settlements in Galilee and Tel-Hai were successfully defended against fierce Arab attack by Hashomer and ex-legionnaires led by Trumpeldor.

In their drive to consolidate and institutionalize the organizational structures of the House of Labour (the Socialist-Zionist movement, occasionally referred to as the HOL), the leadership of Histadrut and the United Labour Party overlooked the importance of security. Only the militants and the kibbutzim recognized the necessity for maintaining a permanent defence organization. While the attack on Tel-Hai awakened the HOL to the significance of a defence capability, they were slow to assume this responsibility and their efforts to wrest control of this function from the leftists were sporadic.

In 1921, the platform of the United Labour Party took stock of the situation and a committee was formed by Eliahu Golomb and Dov Hoz to work for the creation of a defence society. Their task was not an easy one. Soon after the Arab riots of 1920–1921, Hashomer, with the support of dissident former legionnaires, defied the Golomb-Hoz committee and attempted to establish an independent Defence Party, allegedly with the support of the Comintern.[15] Furthermore, a paragraph referring to a "military defence legion" in Histadrut's platform proved unacceptable to pacifists.

The greatest challenge to the defence committee came from

factions of Hashomer and the dissolved Labour Legion who championed a militant defence policy and fortified themselves in some kibbutzim. These militant elements could not be absorbed by the HOL both because it was organizationally unprepared to meet the task of defence, and also because of pressure from the pacifists and fear of takeover.

Eventually, the effective opposition of Hashomer and the Labour Legion was broken[16] and the Secretary General of Histadrut accepted the Golomb-Hoz committee's recommendation to organize the Haganah, the first Jewish underground in Palestine. Thus it could be said that the Haganah, as an organization, came into being on June 25, 1921.

For the Jews in Palestine, the years 1925–1929 were relatively peaceful and prosperous. With large-scale Zionist immigration and negligible Arab nationalist activity, the Haganah had little need to grow. The situation took a turn in 1929, however, when the Arabs attacked Jewish communities in Hevron and Safad and Jewish businesses in Jerusalem and Tel-Aviv. The Mandatory was caught unprepared and the Haganah was not sufficiently developed to defend the Jews effectively. This set of circumstances brought the Haganah into the spotlight of Zionist politics. As David Ben Gurion has reminisced, "I told Dr. Weizmann (in 1929) that the Jerusalem riots of 1920 and the Jaffa massacre of 1921 would be as nothing compared to what we would face in the future."[17] Ben Gurion adds that Dr. Chaim Arlozoroff, then head of the political department of the Jewish Agency, said, "In view of the present circumstances (1930), there is no way to fulfil Zionism without a transition period in which the Jewish minority takes over control of Palestine as an organized revolutionary élite".[18]

The Golomb committee appealed to the World Zionist Congress which met in Geneva, in 1930, for special funds to maintain the Haganah. Colonel Kish, then head of the political department of the Jewish Agency was enlisted to muster support for their request. Their appeal failed, however, largely because many (Bourgeois Zionists) in the Zionist leadership objected to giving Socialists a monopoly on defence.[19] This decision triggered a split within the Histadrut between moderates and former Hashomer militants who desired to break away from World Zionism by forming their own General Conference of Watchmen. Golomb and Ben Gurion succeeded in defeating this proposition within the party, but once again internal factionalism and conflicts between Socialist-Zionism and World Zionism weakened the Haganah.

In the cities the Haganah failed to recruit many of the new immigrants to its ranks. With the exception of a few Haganah units in the cities who were sympathetic to Socialist-Zionism, the Jews, for the most part, remained heavily dependent on the settlement defence structures for their security. From their stronghold in the collectives, Hashomer and ex-members of the Labour Legion continued to challenge the United Labour Party's claim to responsibility for, and control over, the defence of the Jews in Palestine and only they recognized the need for a permanent defence organization.

The Case of the United Kibbutz:
Chief Mobilizer of the Haganah

The pioneer Zionists who entered Palestine in the Third Immigration (1919–1925) had a tremendous impact on the development of the institutional structures of Socialist-Zionism which in effect constituted a state within a state prior to independence.[20] It was this group which transformed the disparate socio-economic and political experiments of the Second Immigration (1904–1905) into an effective and permanent organizational framework. It was through these men that the legacy of the Labour Legion persisted.

This group was instrumental in forming the all-inclusive and powerful Histadrut (1920); in creating a united Israeli labour political party—the United Labour Party (Ahdut Ha-Avoda) (1919) which became the all-powerful Mapai party (1929) which has ruled Palestine-Israel since 1935; in bringing the economic co-operatives under direct labour control—the Workers' Society (Hevrat Ovdim); in spearheading the first kibbutz movement—the United Kibbutz (Ha-Kibbutz ha-Meuchad); in dominating the reservoir of the Socialist-Zionist pioneer (Hehalutz) movement in Eastern Europe; and lastly, instituting the first all-inclusive security organization of the Yishuv in Palestine—the Haganah (Defence).

The pioneer Zionists of the Third Immigration regarded themselves as an élite group, the cadre of Jewish nation-building. In this role they successfully manipulated national symbols via extraordinary social and political mobilization structures. In 1927, some members of this group formed Ha-Kibbutz ha-Meuchad (United Kibbutz Movement also referred to as UKM). In Palestine, this organization came to wield enormous influence, disproportionate to its size, and was responsible for the emergence of a Socialist-Zionist monopoly over the instruments of national fulfilment and self-realization. Most important, however, the UKM was the first Socialist-Zionist group to recognize the need for maintaining vigilant self-defence units and played a major part in organizing and controlling the first effective and sustaining Jewish security forces, the Haganah and its élite professional corps, the Palmach (Shock Platoons). Thus the UKM acted as chief agent for the mobilization of efforts toward nation-building in Israel.

As a self-proclaimed pioneer élite group, the UKM was a minority in the Yishuv, in the Histadrut, and in Mapai (3–4%). However, it succeeded in institutionalizing its objectives by using Mapai and Histadrut to fulfil its universalist mission. With its high commitment, dedication, and sense of moral superiority, the UKM succeeded in penetrating the top levels of all the institutional structures of Socialist-Zionism and dominating the high command of Palmach and the middle echelon of Haganah. For membership, it drew upon the reservoir of labour-Zionists in the Eastern European Diaspora, as well as the Socialist youth movement in Palestine's urban centres.

The most predominant group in the Third Immigration was the Hehalutz (Pioneer) contingent from Eastern Europe. Between 1927 and 1931, the UKM's period of consolidation, over 80% of labour immigration to Palestine came from the pioneer movement. In 1926, 40·6% of the agricultural labourers in this group became affiliated with the UKM,[21] which would account in part for UKM's high degree of cohesiveness.

Kibbutz Ein-Harod, the founder of the UKM, dominated UKM's executive committee. It also penetrated Histadrut's councils, urban workers' councils, and Histadrut's Workers' Society enterprises. At the same time (late 1920s), UKM registered *only* 4·4% of the total membership of Histadrut.[22]

In 1926, out of 31,836 registered Jewish workers, UKM scored 8,692 (or 27%), and by 1937 UKM commanded 42·7%)

of the Jewish labourers in Palestine. As membership increased, so did the number of UKM settlements.

By 1930, two out of seven of Mapai party secretariat were affiliated with the UKM. By 1940, ten out of fifty-two of Histadrut's executive council (Va'ad Ha-poel) were affiliated with UKM, as were one out of four in the executive council of Tnuva (Histadrut's chief distribution co-operative).[23] This was also the case in the Workers' Bank (Bank Ha-poalim) and other Histadrut enterprises.[24]

During the years 1935–1937, a fierce struggle took place between the HOL and revisionist right-wing Zionists. While this was going on, the UKM successfully enlisted the support of Histadrut and Mapai and, in fact, further entrenched itself in the councils and executives of both. In the end, however, Mapai could no longer tolerate the extraordinary pressure exerted by the UKM bloc, which was unwilling to surrender to party discipline, and they split in 1942.

The Palestine Jewish community's Fourth General Assembly elections resulted in 36·8% of the general Yishuv vote going to Mapai, while Faction B (the political arm of the UKM, later the United Labour Party) registered only 9·1% of total Yishuv votes. In the election to the Histadrut's Sixth Convention in January 1945, United Labour received 17·7% of total labour votes and Mapai collected 53·7% of the vote.[25]

A detailed study of municipal elections in 1942 demonstrated an average 57% of the total population voted for Mapai, while only 18% voted for the United Labour Party. Even in the UKM capital, Ein-Harod, Mapai received 56% of the vote, while the United Labour Party came in with 42% of the vote. Only in the UKM's sabra (Israeli-born) dominated kibbutzim of Na'an, Yagur, Beit-Hashita, and Ramat-Hakovesh, did the UKM receive over 75% of the vote.[26]

The appeal of the UKM diminished with the decline of conscious Jewish Socialist immigration and with the final destruction of Eastern European Jewry—when Hehalutz ceased to exist. Since the mid-'thirties, UKM membership constituted no more than 30% of Jewish labourers in Palestine. The main source of new adherents were now the Socialist youth groups and the UKM concentrated on mobilizing these Israeli-born youths to the agricultural settlements. It was this drive to attract Israeli youth to the kibbutzim that accounts for the UKM's extra-ordinary influence in the Haganah. The subsequent creation and development of the Palmach illustrates again the organizational resiliency and cohesiveness of the UKM as a mobilizer of the future élite corps of the Israeli army.

NOTES

1. Zahal is a popular abbreviation for Zva Ha-Haganah Le-Israel (Israel Defence Forces).

2. Vladimir (Zeev) Jabotinsky, was one of the first influential Zionist activists. A rival of Weizmann, he split in 1933 from the World Zionist Movement to create the Revisionist-Zionist organization. For his biography, see Joseph B. Schechtman, *Rebel and Statesman* (New York: Thomas Yoseloff, 1956), 3 vols.

3. Although the majority in Hashomer (including Itzchak Ben Zvi, President of Israel from 1952–1962), did not subscribe to Vilbashevitz-Schochet's doctrines, the minority in Hashomer, by Bolshevik methods, finally took over its Central Executive Committee. See *Sepher Hashomer* (*The Book of Hashomer*) (Heb.), Chapters I and II (Tel-Aviv: Davar, 1936). See also Ben Zion Dinour *et al.* (eds.), *Sepher Toldot Ha-Haganah* (*History of the Haganah*) (Heb.), Vol. II, Part I (Tel-Aviv: Ma'arachot, 1959), pp. 219–41.

4. The paper spoke of the Jewish National Home and the non-Jewish community as being "of equal weight". This was interpreted by Zionists as a turning away from the Balfour Declaration. See Hurewitz, *The Struggle for Palestine* (New York: W. W. Norton, 1950), p. 22.

5. Hurewitz, *ibid.*, pp. 22–23. See also Musa Alami, "The Lesson of Palestine", *The Middle East Journal*, III (October 1949), pp. 373–405. (This is a condensation of his Ibrat Filastin, published in Beirut in March 1949.) See also Paul L. Hanna, *British Policy in Palestine* (Washington, D.C.: American Council on Public Affairs, 1942); M. F. Abcarius, *Palestine through the Fog of Propaganda* (London: 1946); and Ya'aqov Shimoni, "The Arabs and the Approaching War with Israel", *Hamizrah Hehadash* (*The New East*), No. 47 (Jerusalem, 1962), pp. i–ix.

6. The Fifth Poale Zion Congress which met on July 20 in Vienna. Hashomer was officially dissolved, and beginning on June 18, 1920, it became active in the Labour Legion and formed a faction in 1926 called Ha-Kibbutz (The Kibbutz) within the Labour Legion. See Dinour, *History of Haganah, Vol. I, II, ibid.*, pp. 219–41.

7. Dinour, *History of Haganah, ibid.*, Vol. I, Part II (1956), pp. 437–40; Bracha Habas and Eliezer Schochet, *Sepher Ha-Aliya Ha-Shnia* (*The Book of the Second Immigration*) (Heb.) (Tel-Aviv: Am Oved, 1947); John H. Patterson, *With the Judeans in the Palestinian Campaign* (London, 1922); David Ben Gurion, *Ketavim* (*Works*) (Heb.) (Tel-Aviv: Mapai, 1949), Vol. I.

8. A view of the Legion and the left is found in Joseph Trumpeldor's *Letters* (Tel-Aviv: Am Oved, 1946); see also Dinour, *History of Haganah, op. cit.*, Vol. I, Part II, pp. 639–67.

9. General Allenby, Commander of the Palestine Military Occupation, as well as his military staff, stood firmly opposed to Jabotinsky's proposals. See Dinour, *History of Haganah, op. cit.*, pp. 517–20, 535, 549. See Jabotinsky's letter to Chaim Weizmann (1915), Weizmann Archives; also Chaim

Weizmann, *Trial and Error: An Autobiography* (New York: Harpers, 1949).
10. Zeine N. Zeine, *Arab–Turkish Relations and the Emergence of Arab Nationalism* (Beirut: Khayats', 1958), pp. 73–75; also Hurewitz, *The Struggle*, pp. 55–60.

11. Moshe Braslavsky, *Tnuat Ha-Poalim Ha-Eretz Israelit (The Palestine Labor Movement)* (Heb.) Vol. I (Tel-Aviv: Ha-Kibbutz ha-Meuchad, 1955–1956), pp. 185–92.

12. Histadrut and Ahdut Ha-Avoda founding conferences (1920), accepted responsibilities for organizing "Defence and Watchmanship of the Yishuv in Palestine".

13. Ben Gurion, *Mema'amad le-Am (From Class to Nation)* (Heb.) (Tel-Aviv: Ayanot, 1954), p. 379.

14. Berl Katznelson, *Ketavim (Works)* (Heb.), S. Yavnieli (ed.), 12 vols. (Tel-Aviv: Ayanot, Mapai Publishing House, 1947–1955), Vol. I.

15. Dinour, *History of Haganah*, *op. cit.*, Vol. I, Part I (1954), pp. 128–31.

16. The extreme militants left later for the Soviet Union in 1926. The rest accepted the authority of the Histadrut. Later others led by Yitzhak Tabenkin (see later pages) organized the first kibbutz movement (Ha-Kibbutz ha-Meuchad—United Kibbutz Movement) in 1927 in Ein-Harod.

17. Historical Branch of Zahal, *Toldot Milhemet Ha-Komemiout (History of the War of Liberation)* (Heb.) (Tel-Aviv: Ma'arachot, 1959), p. 13.

18. Chaim Arlozoroff, *Jerusalem Diary* (Heb.) (Tel-Aviv: Mapai, 1932), p. 341, quoted in *History of the War of Liberation*, *op. cit.*, p. 14.

19. Despite the semi-official *History of Haganah* (or *Sepher Toldot Ha-Haganah*, published by the Ministry of Defence) attempt to conceal and thus partially reveal the failure of Labour's leadership to comprehend the crucial role of defence, we must conclude that *some* efforts have been made in this direction.

20. On the extraordinary role of Zionist immigration in Palestine and its sociological structure see S. N. Eisenstadt, *The Absorption of Immigrants* (London: Routledge & Kegan Paul, 1954); also see Braslavsky, *Palestine Labor Movement*, *op. cit.*, pp. 161–282.

21. D. Weintraub, M. Lissak, and Y. Atzmon, *The Chequered Cloth* (New York: Cornell University Press, forthcoming 1968), manuscript page 302.

22. *Ibid.*, p. 308; see also Moshe Basok (ed.), *The Book of Hehalutz* (Heb.) (Jerusalem: The Jewish Agency, 1940); and Braslavsky, *Palestine Labor Movement*, *op. cit.*, pp. 381–82.

23. *Ibid.*, Weintraub, *Chequered Cloth*, MS. p. 323.

24. *Ibid.*, pp. 332–37; Amos Perlmutter, "Ideology and Organization: The Politics of Socialistic Parties in Israel, 1897–1957", unpub. diss., Berkeley: University of California, 1957, pp. 321–41.

25. *Ibid.*, tables 1 and 2, pp. 334–35.

26. *Ibid.*, p. 336.

CHAPTER II

The Arab Revolt:
Catalyst of Haganah Expansion

THE publication of the Passfield White Paper, in 1930, marked the end of a period (1925–1929) of relative tranquillity and prosperity in Palestine. The Mandatory became more precise regarding its attitude toward the emergence of a Jewish National Home and recommended stricter land transfer and immigration controls.[1] This was interpreted by the more militant Jewish leaders, especially Jabotinsky and his followers, as revoking the Balfour Delaration. This change in the Mandatory's attitude came at a time when the Arab nationalist movement in Palestine was gathering momentum and was radicalized by the fundamentalist and extremist, al-Hajj Amin, the mufti of Jerusalem. Both developments constituted a formidable challenge to the Yishuv's aspirations toward nationhood.

The turn toward extremists and desperadoes by the Arab nationalist movement in Palestine can be attributed to several factors: the feudal and transitional nature of the Arab community, the growth and success of the Jewish community but, above all, to Arab opposition to the Mandatory.[2]

The Arab Revolt (1936–1939) began with a general strike which quickly collapsed, continued with riots and terrorism directed against Jewish settlements, and ended as a furious but futile revolt against Great Britain. This first large-scale all-Arab nationalist insurrection ended in despair due to fratricidal rivalries between several Arab nationalist leaders. Its failure must be laid to al-Hajj Amin whose personal ambition to dominate the Arab community in Palestine entangled this fragile Arab nationalist movement in a hopeless struggle against the powerful resources of the Mandatory.

C

Although these were years of growing strength for the economic, social, and political efforts of the Yishuv, the Arab Revolt and the concurrent British withdrawal of support for the principles of the Balfour Declaration divided the Yishuv on the issue of self-defence. The problem was twofold: what form of resistance should the Jews adopt toward the Mandatory and what type of defence should they support against the Arabs.

For the Yishuv, the Arab Revolt worked as a catalyst. The advocates of a permanent defence organization now had a stronger argument to convince the Yishuv's highest authorities and World Zionist leaders of the need for a Jewish army, independent of the Mandatory and ready to meet the Arab challenge. While these conditions favoured the development of a strong Jewish defence force, they left the Arab community impotent and unprepared to meet the double challenge it had set for itself, the ousting of the British and the surrender of the Jewish community in Palestine.

Awareness and criticism of British sympathy for the Arab cause mounted in Jewish Palestine after 1930. The last official British statement on Palestine was contained in a letter sent to Dr. Weizmann from Prime Minister Ramsay MacDonald on December 30, 1931, in which he expressly reaffirmed both the article and the Preamble of the Mandate and again recognized that the Mandate was undertaken on behalf of the Jewish people and *not just the Jewish population in Palestine*.[3] The subsequent silence of the British, however, created a climate of political uncertainty which kept the Arab and Jewish communities in a perpetual state of tension. By early 1936 the situation had become highly volatile. As one writer described it:

One contributory factor was the Mandatory's latest recommendation for a Legislative Council, which was still an unsettled matter early in April when the Colonial Office invited the Arab spokesman to send a delegation to London for further discussion.

On April 15, two Jews were murdered by Arabs, and in the next few days there were suspected Jewish reprisals as well as assaults on Arabs in Tel Aviv and on Jews in Jaffa. Arab nationalists in Nablus created a National Committee for that city on April 20. Before the month passed similar committees appeared in all towns of concentrated Arab population and in some of the larger villages.[4]

Soon after this the Arab Higher Committee was founded. It included the leaders of both the Independence Party and the Arab Nationalist Party, of which the latter was led by the grand mufti al-Hajj Amin. The first act of the Higher Committee was to call for a general strike, by means of which they sought to exert pressure on the Mandatory to suspend Jewish immigration and to abandon the principles of the Balfour Declaration.

The British Mandatory viewed the mounting crisis with apprehension and appointed a Royal Commission, known as the Peel Commission, to study the causes underlying the "disturbances". The Commission published a report on July 7, 1935, in which

It stated unequivocally that the Arab grievances about Jewish immigration, Jewish land acquisition, and the Mandatory's failure to develop self-governing institutions cannot be regarded as legitimate under the terms of the Mandate.... The Palestine Mandate, it was observed, was originally premised on the assumption that the Arabs would acquiesce in the establishment of the Jewish National Home because of the material advantages. But no mutual understanding had been achieved.[5]

The Commission further argued that

Arab nationalism is as intense a force as Jewish. The Arab leaders' demand for national self-government and the shutting down of the Jewish National Home has remained unchanged since 1920. Like Jewish nationalism, Arab nationalism is stimulated by the educational system and by the growth of the Youth movement. It has also been greatly encouraged by the recent Anglo-Egyptian and Franco-Syrian treaties. The gulf between the races is thus already wide and will continue to widen if the present Mandate is maintained.[6]

The Commission concluded that Palestine should be partitioned into three sections, one comprising a Jewish state, one an Arab state, and one remaining under the authority of the Mandatory. The proposed Jewish state was to encompass the Galilee, the Jezreel Valley, and the coastal plain to a point midway between Gaza and Jaffa—which, all told, amounted to about one-fifth of the total Mandate area. The partition proposal divided Jewry into two factions, those who were for and those who were against it, and the controversy came up for discussion at the 20th Zionist Congress in Zurich in 1937. Dr. Weizmann and the moderate wing of the general Zionists, and Ben Gurion and the moderate left (with the exception of Berl Katznelson) favoured partition. They were prepared to exchange territorial claims and the uncertainties of continued Mandatory administration for the benefits of early self-rule in an amputated Palestine.

On the whole, the Zionist Congress regarded the Royal Commission Report as acceptable. By a vote of 299 to 160 it endorsed the attempts made by the British to resolve the crisis, but it did not endorse the principle of partition. This ambivalent attitude toward partition was also reflected within the labour movement, and the controversy soon took the form of internal party conflicts in Palestine.

Ben Gurion advocated the concept of a Jewish Commonwealth, and it was for reasons of expediency in achieving this end that he was willing to accept the idea of an amputated Palestine. His constant public plea was for a Jewish National Home as a "state on the way". During the 1930s, especially, his speeches before Mapai, Histadrut, and the Royal Commission emphasized the immediate need for the establishment of a Jewish state.

> Exile is complete dependence—in material things, in politics, in culture, in ethics, and in intellect. . . . They are dependent on who constitute an alien minority, who have no Homeland and are separated from their origins, from the soil, from labor and from economic activity. So we must become the captains of our fortunes. . . . We must become independent.[7]

Ben Gurion saw the state as a shelter for the organized community, an institution giving the community freedom of action and mobility: "We are a Jewish Community which is in fact a Jewish Commonwealth in the making."[8] He thus equated the ideology and structure of Palestinian Zionism with the sort of state that seemed most nearly possible.

The urgent need for establishing a state, in Ben Gurion's analysis, arose from three factors: (1) the deterioration of the Mandate; (2) the growth of Arab nationalism; and (3) the need for an open immigration policy in view of the holocaust that was befalling Jewry in Central Europe and Germany. He believed that a state, no matter what its size, would solve the compelling problems then facing Zionism. His antagonists in Mapai, and within Zionism generally, agreed that these three factors constituted the core of the problem, but they could not accept his conclusion that partition was the answer. Ben Gurion's opponents objected, in particular, to the small size of the commonwealth proposed by the Royal Commission. As Yitzchak Tabenkin (the ideologue of the UKM) put it somewhat ironically: "We shall have a state—we shall call it Tel Aviv State!"

The Royal Commission Plan apportioned only 20% of the total area of Palestine to the Jewish commonwealth. At best, this would mean that the commonwealth would become a small canton dependent upon the Arab East for its economic survival. This did not discourage Ben Gurion, however, for, as he saw it, the only way to gain initial independence from Britain and the Arab majority was through partition. The Arab Revolt, the rise of Hitler, and the withering away of the Balfour principles convinced him that independence had to come soon, and that a minimum solution should therefore be accepted.

Tabenkin and other fervent labour-Zionists favoured an entirely different approach to achieving statehood. They advocated a last frontier concept whereby the size of the future state would be determined entirely by the scope of a border settlement programme and not by political bargaining. Under the protection of the Mandatory, a circle of kibbutzim could take root in the western basin of the Jordan which was, at that time, thinly populated. The kibbutzim would strengthen the economic foundations of the future state and would eventually come to dominate both the Yishuv and Zionism. At the United Kibbutz Movement Conference held at Beit-Hashita in July 1937, he declared war against partition, explaining:

The Jewish state will be attained through a large-scale colonization program of all parts of Eretz Israel (Palestine)

... and also through the perpetual strength of the Jewish catastrophe as an international political factor.[9]

Berl Katznelson, Mapai's chief ideologue, accepted neither Ben Gurion's nor Tabenkin's views on partition. He opposed partition primarily because he feared the growing strength of the Arab nationalist movements, and thought that new political constellations in the Near East, based on growing sympathies between Nazis, Fascists, and some Arab nationalists, might threaten any independent state, small or large. He also suspected that pro-Arab elements in the British government favoured partition because it would leave the Jews to be strangled in an impossibly small territory, which would then fall into Arab hands.

To Katznelson, partition meant a majority Arab state and a minority Jewish state, which he regarded as an untenable situation. At a conference in Zurich in August 1937, he said:

> I do not claim that what is good for the Arabs and for the British is bad for us all. But our political thinking must shy away from the idea that we receive anything for nothing. We exist, here, one cannot get rid of us without offering us some compensation. *The Mandate also exists*, and has become a somewhat uncomfortable instrument for England. And because the Mandate is in force they offer us a state or something like a state. It is a fact that the Mandate exists, even if its promises have been weakened considerably. If there were no Mandate, even such a plan (partition) would not have been offered to us. Therefore, let us remember ... let us not defy the Mandate, let us not aid those who wish its abandonment.[10]

For the duration of the Arab Revolt and riots against the Mandatory, in 1936–1939, the Yishuv and its biggest bloc, the HOL, led by Ben Gurion, pursued a policy of restraint toward the Mandatory. Perceiving the futility of the Arab Revolt, the Jews sought to turn it to their advantage. The Jewish leadership knew that if they adopted the same strategy as the Arabs against the Mandatory it would end in catastrophe, for once the Mandatory were overthrown they would be left alone to face the Arabs which at that time would have been disastrous.

Thus they followed a course of moderation which dictated co-operation with the Mandatory and self-defence against the Arabs.

Recognizing the reluctance of the British to defend their settlements against Arab attack, the Jews used the situation as an excuse for buttressing their own defence forces. Working closely with the British, Zionist moderates were able to develop a clandestine Jewish army protected by the Mandatory but not responsible to it. Thus they were able both to contain the Arabs and establish the defence apparatus which one day would help them to achieve nationhood.

The chief proponent of restraint (havlagah) was Dr. Weizmann, the President of the World Zionist Organization, and he was supported in this by the majority of Zionist leaders in Palestine. There was opposition, however, voiced mainly by members of the younger generation, especially those born in Palestine. These young rebels, viewed restraint as a form of capitulation to the British and they championed a strategy of active resistance (maavak) to the Mandatory, a war against the imperialists in much the same vein as the Arabs. These young men were to be found mainly in Jabotinsky's Beitar youth movement and had little say in the political decisions of the Yishuv. Since the advocates of restraint were part of the Socialist-Zionist power structure, and thus were more influential, this, at first, became the official doctrine of the Yishuv, of Socialist-Zionism and their instrument, Haganah.

Following a course of restraint imposed a severe burden on the Jewish community in Palestine which was under constant attack by Arab terrorists. This, compounded with the attitude of the Mandatory administration, which was indifferent, and London's policy of appeasing the Arabs only strengthened the position of the rebels.

The first break from the official policy came from within Haganah where a militant group formed what it called Haganah B. Initially, the leaders of Haganah B did not want to align themselves with any political party but found it difficult to maintain a neutral position on such politically explosive matters. Eventually the poet-intellectual Avraham Stern, an independent Revisionist and leader of Beitar, split from the Haganah, and recruited members of Haganah B into a militant and terrorist organization called the National Military Organization (Irgun Zvai Leumi, also known as "the Stern Gang", but hereafter identified by its initials, NMO).

For its goals, the NMO looked to Jabotinsky for inspiration and carried his ideas to their logical conclusion. Jabotinsky gathered to his banner a large number of disaffected elements, who devoted themselves to the thorough revision of Zionist leadership, tactics, and programme. They were critical of the "old" Zionists, the power structure of the Jewish state within the Mandatory, who, they asserted, no longer spoke for "the whole or even the majority of Zionist Jewry".

The Revisionists talked about "liquidating the Diaspora" and populating Palestine and Transjordan with eight to eighteen million people. Jabotinsky envisioned a Mandatory policy unequivocally directed toward implementing a rapid mass migration of Jews to Palestine. He opposed the autonomous organization of a Jewish self-defence corps under the Mandate, because he insisted that it must be organized by the Mandate government, made subordinate to its officers, and operated under its immediate authority and direction.

Jabotinsky reasoned that if the Jews undertook to defend, educate, and colonize themselves, this would only make it easier for the Mandatory to avoid responsibility for creating the Jewish state. For the sake of these goals, the Revisionists were prepared to consider expendable the autonomous institutions of the Jews in Palestine and, in the last analysis, the community itself.

What appealed to the rebels in the NMO was Jabotinsky's fervour and militarism, but they took his ideas one step further than he was willing to go. Whereas he favoured working within the organizational framework of the Mandatory, the young militants realized the impossibility of achieving mass immigration by collaborating with an administration whose government had explicitly limited immigration. Thus they operated outside the authority of both the Mandatory and the Yishuv and never secured more than reluctant support from Jabotinsky and almost no guidance since he was exiled by the British in 1936.[11]

The NMO was a strictly military organization whose members were professional revolutionaries undisciplined by part or ideology.[12] Members of Beitar formed a political committee and attempted to govern the NMO but actual power was held by its General Staff, led by Avraham Stern who was Secretary General. Revisionist Zionists disapproved of Stern's terrorist methods, but Stern's General Staff simply became independent of Revisionism and pursued its own policies.

Stern attacked the concept of partition as no more than a palliative and became the first apostle of total resistance to the Mandatory. His contempt for the official line of the Yishuv, Histadrut, and Haganah was expressed in an open clash with Haganah in Jerusalem. Although the NMO precipitated the clash by stealing armaments from a Haganah munitions centre, this incident was only one of the grievances which set Haganah against it. Basically, the NMO's political irresponsibility jeopardized the whole Zionist cause and threatened to turn world public opinion against them. Thus the NMO constituted far more of a threat to the Yishuv than it did toward the Mandatory.

Lacking the support of his Revionist mentors, Stern eventually was relegated to the periphery of Zionist politics, but his call for military resistance to the Mandatory was far from ineffective. When the Mandatory hung the teenage Beitar leader Shlomo Ben-Yoseph,[13] against the advice of the Yishuv's leadership and in spite of Jabotinsky's efforts to gain a commutation of his sentence from the Colonial Minister, Malcolm MacDonald, Stern's group gained the adherence of much of Jabotinsky's youth movement and its Jerusalem commander David Raziel, a graduate of the Hebrew University and a leader of the militant student group, El-Al.[14] Neither Raziel nor Stern would accept a compromise offer from Haganah, and civil war seemed close.

But a temporary truce was worked out by Israel Rokach, the mayor of Tel-Aviv, and the two groups agreed to terms of co-operation under which Raziel was granted the use of some of Haganah's funds and facilities. Jabotinsky, who had been urged by Golomb to unite the groups, gave his approval. But the agreement found a fierce opponent in the person of Ben Gurion, Secretary General of the Jewish Agency and leader of Mapai. Ben Gurion was firmly committed to the principle of unity and demanded total adherence to the policy of restraint which he advocated. As he would later in the *Altalena* affair of

1948, and presiding over the dissolution of Palmach in 1948, Ben Gurion insisted that the defence function remain subordinated to the leadership of the Yishuv and of Zionism.

The most effective opposition to Ben Gurion's "defeatist" policies came from the emerging first generation of Palestinian-born youth active in Mapai and in the kibbutz movement. They engineered a struggle for control of Socialist-Zionism which pitted the leadership of Mapai and Histadrut, headed by Ben Gurion, against members of the left kibbutz movement, led by Tabenkin, his chief rival.

The conflict between the two leaders culminated in 1935, when Ben Gurion concluded a labour pact with the Revisionist leader, Jabotinsky, which included an important proviso concerning the allocation of quotas for Jewish immigration to Palestine.[15] The Passfield White Paper had restricted the number of Jews permitted to enter Palestine and Jabotinsky wanted a share of the quota in order to tap his own reservoirs in the Diaspora and elsewhere. Tabenkin and other militant Socialists were outraged by Ben Gurion's action which they regarded as a betrayal of Socialist-Zionism. Tabenkin argued that the kibbutz was not simply a form of settlement but a way of life, the *raison d'être* of Zionism. In his view, the Socialist settlement system performed the primary function in Palestine and the political parties had only a limited role in the development of class and nation.[16] Ben Gurion, on the other hand, regarded all Jews as the same. He held that the Jews constituted a nation (am) and not a class (ma'amad) and that Mapai, as the party responsible for the "state on the way", represented the nation and not an individual class. It was the settlement system which gradually assumed the major function of guiding and protecting the rebels who advocated stiff resistance against the Arabs. This group was destined to become the second generation of Haganah leaders and the nucleus of the Israel Defence Army.

The riots of 1936 made it clear to most Jewish leaders that Arab nationalism would no longer confine its efforts to isolated acts of terrorism, and that its operations in Palestine were being supported financially by Arab leaders in Syria, Iraq, and Jordan. The Yishuv also grew more concerned with making military preparations for defence against new Arab assaults, and its governing body, the Jewish National Council, was allowed to organize a police force, the Notrim (Guards). This "legal" military unit was acknowledged by many, however, as not enough. On this point, Ben Gurion and Jabotinsky agreed, and successfully argued the case of self-defence before the World Zionist Congress at Geneva in 1936. Funds from the World Zionist Organization were allocated for the increased purchase of arms and weapons and for an elaborate, large-scale programme to train Palestinian youth as the core of a future army.

Haganah was reorganized under the auspices of Histadrut, and by paying full-time salaries to Shaul Meirov and other Haganah leaders, and by recruiting volunteers from its rank and file for week-end and spare-time training, Histadrut once again assumed the task of defence organization and co-ordination. Operating out of room 33 in Beit Brenner, the Histadrut House in Tel-Aviv, Haganah became an embryo ministry of defence. One of Meirov's innovations, in addition to the establishment of a regular defence budget, was the formation of an Information Office. The Information Office included an Arab Office, which secured information from Arab leaders; it gave Haganah control of what amounted to a nascent intelligence office, which determined much of the Jewish community's Arab policy.

The 1930s were years of growing power for Socialist-Zionism (in 1935, it gained close to 45% of the Yishuv Assembly, thereby joining American Zionism as a decisive force in World Zionism). Concurrently, the organizational growth of Histadrut was greatly enhanced by the rise of Haganah, the defence establishment it sustained and sheltered.

Although Haganah's constitution proclaimed that it was "a general Yishuv confederation which *in all of its activities* stands above class and party and is only responsible to the higher national authorities",[17] this claim was never borne out in practice. Haganah was allied with Socialist-Zionism from the beginning, and (in the 1930s) its growing organizational connections with Mapai (the controlling party in Histadrut since 1930) brought on the first serious split within Haganah.

Because Socialist-Zionism held singular responsibility for defence the institutional and organizational structures of Haganah naturally followed patterns developed by its Socialist-

Zionist creators. Haganah was not a step-level function but a pattern-maintenance sub-system of the general system (Histadrut); it assumed an instrumental state-making function, and its organizational structure reflected the aims and ideology of Mapai. Despite the fact that it was a clandestine and limited operation, Haganah became a major institution in the entire Yishuv social system.

It is not surprising that Histadrut's political critics called Haganah "a state within a state"; it was (in fact) a political institution, with institutional leaders and a professional staff, as were all Socialist-Zionist vehicles for advancing the development of a Jewish Socialist commonwealth. On the other hand, it never became—despite its "above parties" claim—an independent professional military underground. But because it was controlled and directed by the Socialist-Zionist movement, who provided its leadership, and because it served the interests of the Yishuv, it neither grew into a professional military clique nor created an officer class élite.

As a closer examination is made of the political behaviour of the Israeli army, it should be remembered that Golomb and other founders of Haganah believed that Zionism could "not be accomplished by force". Although he also held that nationhood could not be achieved "without an independent Jewish Force", the reasons were not really military. They were dictated by "political necessity", and the psychological and cultural need "to turn the oppressed Jew of the Diaspora into an independent Hebrew in his homeland".[18]

The Arab Revolt was a prelude to the Jewish War of Liberation (1947–1949). It alerted the Yishuv to the need to consolidate politically and, above all, to turn Haganah into a permanent and independent Jewish force, the nucleus of the Jewish army which fought to victory in 1948. The tragedy of the revolt by the Arabs in Palestine is that while they called the challenge, the Jews called the terms.

The Arab rebellion could have turned into a Jewish massacre but for the mufti's fatal mistake of directing the action primarily against the Mandatory instead of against the Jews. This *forced* the Mandatory to rely on armed Jewish force in addition to its own troops and police to crush the revolt. Without initial British support and protection, the Yishuv would have been at the mercy of the Arab terrorists and there probably would have been no contest in 1948.

NOTES

1. For the story of the Passfield White Paper see Hurewitz, *The Struggle, op. cit.*, p. 22.

2. This is not the place to analyse in detail the Palestinian Arab nationalist movement. To date, there are no serious studies of this aspect of Arab nationalism. For material available, see *ibid.*, pp. 51–80, 112–23; for an Arab nationalist interpretation, see George Antonius, *The Arab Awakening* (New York: Capricorn Books, 1965), pp. 387–412; for the Jewish interpretation, see Michael Assaf, *The Arab Awakening and Their Departure* (Heb.) (Tel-aviv: Davar, 1967), pp. 123–53. Two outstanding essays are Yehuda Bauer, "Riots or Revolt", *Ha-Aretz* (April 15, 1966), pp. 9, 12; and Shimoni, "The Arabs", *op cit.*, pp. i–ix. The Afro–Asian Institute of the University of Tel-Aviv is now engaged in a large-scale study on Palestine Arab nationalist movement. In the absence of the documents of the mandatory administration in Palestine no adequate study of the British attitude toward Arabs and Zionists is as yet possible.

3. Bernard Joseph (Yoseph), *British Rule in Palestine* (Washington: Public Affairs Office, 1948), p. 135.

4. Hurewitz, *The Struggle, op. cit.*, p. 67.

5. *Ibid.*, p. 73.

6. Palestine Royal Commission Report, *Summary* (London: Her Majesty's Stationery Office, July 1937), pp. 6–7.

7. Ben Gurion, *Rebirth and Destiny of Israel* (Mordekhai Nurock ed. and tr.) (New York: Philosophical Library, 1954), p. 137.

8. *Ibid.*, p. 201.

9. Yitzhak Tabenkin, "History of Ha-Kibbutz ha-Meuchad", *Mebefnim (Inside)* (Heb.) (July 1937), VII, pp. 9, 16.

10. Katznelson, *Ketavim, op. cit.*, Vol. XII, pp. 356, 358.

11. See Hurewitz, *The Struggle, op. cit.*, and Ben Halpern, *The Idea of the Jewish State* (Cambridge: Harvard University Press, 1961). Dinour, *History of Haganah, op. cit.*, (1959), pp. 158–64.

12. Dinour, *History of Haganah, op. cit.*, Vol. II, Part I, Chapters 32 and 33, and Vol. II, Part II, Chapters 54 and 55.

13. On Shlomo Ben-Yoseph, see *ibid.*, David Niv, *Battle for Freedom; The Irgun Zvai Leumi* (Heb.), Vol. I, Part One, pp. 242–78, and Vol. II, Part Two, pp. 61–94 (Tel-Aviv: Klausner Institute, 1965).

14. Both Stern and Raziel were university students and although Socialist-Zionism was a movement led by intellectuals, its influence among the radical students at the Hebrew University was meagre.

15. The Mandatory policy, since 1936, followed a quota system which restricted Jewish immigration to Palestine. The Certificates were given to the Jewish Agency who, on the basis of parity (between political parties), divided the Certificates. This caused bitter feelings among the Zionist parties since Socialist-Zionist immigrants were generally given preference over others.

16. Tabenkin, "History of Ha-Kibbutz ha-Meuchad", *op. cit.*, pp. 230, 235.

17. Dinour, *History of Haganah, op. cit.*, Vol. II, Part I, p. 124.

18. *Ibid.*

CHAPTER III

The "Academies" of the Future Israeli Army

In 1937, under the leadership of Yitzhak (Sandoberg) Sadeh, the Haganah adopted a more militant position, which attracted the rebels of the Hityashvut and kibbutz movements. The new doctrine was, as Sadeh put it: "Don't wait for the Arab marauder. Don't wait to defend the kibbutz. Go after him, move on to the offensive."[1]

With Sadeh's creation of the Patrol (Ha-Nodedet), the first military unit composed of kibbutz youth, Haganah took the offensive and began retaliatory attacks on centres of Arab terrorism. After 1937, Haganah operated as the general staff or nucleus of a large-scale army which was recruited in the kibbutzim, in the privately owned and operated settlements, and in the cities. It organized centres for officer training, improved communications within the kibbutzim system, and published professional military literature. It organized an intensive *Rechesh* (a clandestine supply and weaponry purchasing operation), established a small armament industry, and created the nucleus of a navy and air force. Most important, it set up a far-flung and efficient network for gathering intelligence and information, the *Shay*. It conducted periodic national fund-raising campaigns and distributed literature to its growing membership, thus combining effective communication with the use of the organizational structures and weapons of Socialist-Zionism.

Sadeh's Patrol found ever wider uses in the field. A completely new system of kibbutzim was established between 1937 and 1939 to match the increasing demands of security. Under the impact of a great influx of youth, the kibbutzim and settlements were transformed into a large-scale defence network, each kibbutz with its own fortress and tower guarded by patrols patterned after those founded by Sadeh. The kibbutz now became the home, protector, and guide of Haganah's second generation, and first-born Israelis.

The Special Night Squads (hereafter referred to as SNS), organized and led by Captain Orde Wingate,[2] an irregular British officer, provided another reservoir of Haganah leadership. Wingate, an adventurer of the same stripe as "Chinese" Gordon and Lawrence of Arabia, viewed himself as something of a modern Gideon. Although serving the Mandatory, it was he who argued the case for a Jewish army and finally persuaded the moderate Zionist leadership to accept the idea.[3] Then he met with Haganah intelligence officers and proposed the formation of night squads, whose function would be to train Palestinian youth to destroy centres of Arab terrorism and to create the nucleus of a Jewish army. His recruits, like Sadeh's, came chiefly from the agrarian collectives where he was warmly welcomed and eventually acquired the status of a hero. Among the great numbers of Wingate's volunteers who later became high-ranking officers in the Israel Defence Army, two were outstanding: Maj.-General Moshe Dayan, Chief of Staff between 1953 and 1957, hero of the Sinai Campaign, and Defence Minister since June 1967; and Brig.-General Yigal Allon, commander of the Shock Platoons and of the Southern Front during the Israeli War of Liberation.

The year 1939 brought to an end the policy of limited political co-operation between Haganah and the Mandatory. A White Paper issued by the Mandatory, in the middle of 1939, appeared to recognize and support the basic claims of the Arab nationalists. This heralded the end of the "partition policy of palliatives", and the Colonial Office turned openly against the Jewish community. By restricting the immigration of European Jewish refugees to Palestine and by prohibiting Jewish land purchases, the Mandatory crushed the hopes of those in Palestine who had advocated collaboration.

The way was now open to the militants and activists in both the NMO and Haganah to challenge the policy of restraint. This trend, like most others that fateful year, lasted only until the British–French declaration of war against Germany on September 1, 1939. On September 3, 1939, President Weizmann announced the support of the Jewish people of Palestine for the Allied war effort. This opened another short but fruitful era for the expansion of Jewish defence forces.

Ben Gurion and the Jewish Agency called upon Jews to

enlist in the British Army, and eventually over 30,000 volun-
teered to serve with the Allied forces. The kibbutz movement
and its rebel leadership, however, feared that the Arabs would
take advantage of the war to improve their position in Palestine.
Yigal Allon argued: "A force protecting the Jewish community
in Palestine is necessary. The Jewish community's best men are
fighting on a variety of fronts far from home and protection of
the Yishuv may not be forthcoming since the Mandatory has
not relinquished its White Paper policy."[4] To meet the tasks
set out by Allon, the Haganah committee created the Palmach,
a commando force, in May 1941.

The rise of the Palmach took place in the midst of the most
critical period of Jewish–Mandatory political relationships.
Whereas Hashomer and the battalions were designed to fufil
temporary, specific, and limited military functions, they were
also political organizations with political objectives and
eventually dissolved mainly due to political feuds. The Palmach, by contrast, was conceived as a permanent military unit
with strictly military functions. This was, however, modified
in view of the role played by UKM and the growing frustration
of Jewish youth with the Mandatory.

Between 1939 and 1941 the organization of Haganah was at
its lowest ebb.[5] The UKM–Haganah leadership and the
General Headquarters had practically halted activities and
effective defence declined. This situation stemmed from a bitter
political controversy then raging among the Yishuv leadership,
but especially among the Socialists, on the proper role of Jewish
military structures. During the 1920s, security organizations
were traditionally dissolved when their limited functions of
watchmanship and protection of the kibbutzim were no longer
needed. Since they were clothed with political purposes, their
dissolution affected the HOL more than it did the defensive
posture of the Yishuv. With the convergence of Arab nationalism, the Nazi rise to power in Europe, and Mandatory reluctance
to protect Jewish property and settlements, however, the Jewish
defence units could no longer be dissolved on behalf of greater
unity in the HOL or settling disputes between the Yishuv's
contending political factions on the left and on the right.[6]

Thus the role of labour's most cohesive and best organized
group, the UKM, became crucial. The challenge to the Jewish

Agency's policy of restraint and Haganah's leadership attitude toward a permanent and professional Jewish defence group came from two directions, one from the HOL on the left, and the other from the Revisionist Zionists on the right.[6]

The struggle was brought to a head over the White Paper policy inaugurated by the British in 1939. The problem was to determine whether Haganah should be directed to acquiesce in, or resist, this unmistakably anti-Yishuv policy. The Mandatory actually decided the matter for them when it launched a full-scale campaign to curtail and eventually eliminate independent Jewish military power.[7] This action was primarily in retaliation against the anti-Mandatory terrorist activities of the NMO Revisionists and the Stern Group, who by their deeds had renounced Jabotinsky's idea of a "legal-Haganah" protected and recognized by the Mandatory.

The moderate Zionists in Mapai and Haganah became concerned lest the terrorist activities of the extreme right ruin the thin fabric of co-operation between the Jewish community and the Mandatory. To conciliate the Mandatory, Haganah called for a war against Jewish terrorism. Then commenced the short but infamous Sezon era (1944–1945) when Haganah informed the Mandatory intelligence authorities in Palestine on Jewish terrorists. Mandatory intelligence *failed*, however, to distinguish (probably intentionally) between "legitimate" and terrorist Jewish military power and, at the end of 1946, arrested members of the Haganah. But despite this, Jewish–Mandatory co-operation in the military field prevailed. This was due to a new circumstance—a common enemy in the Nazis.

The Palmach: Haganah's Elite Corps

The commanders of Ha-Nodedet and the SNS and the youth in the kibbutzim and agrarian settlements opposed the Haganah and Yishuv posture of conciliation and co-operation with the Mandatory. They were bitter that SNS and other small, but independent, Jewish military units created in the wake of the Arab Revolt had been dissolved when the crisis passed. The UKM and especially Yitzhak Sadeh, commander of Ha-Nodedet and chief security officer of the SNS, resolved to press for the establishment of a *permanent* and *independent* Jewish *professional* élite corps around which a future permanent and

D

independent army could be built. Sadeh prevailed upon and won the support of Golomb, the commander of Haganah, and Dr. Moshe Sneh, its Chief of Staff, who appointed him General Staff Officer for Palmach at Haganah headquarters.

From its inception, Palmach was designed as an élite and professional corps of Haganah and not as a *sectarian* kibbutz military structure, although it was to draw heavily from the kibbutzim both for men and morale. As a consequence, Palmach became not only Israel's first élite corps but also a role expansionist and ideologically motivated military structure imbued with a sense of mission directed toward national fulfilment.

The Palmach was the first full-time professional military unit of Haganah, which, except for its general staff, was composed of part-time volunteers. Its importance as the intellectual and organizational training ground for the future élite of the Israel Defence Army can be seen quickly in the later careers of its members. Of the twelve general staff brigadiers, during the War of Liberation (there was only one major-general, the Commander-in-Chief General Dori), three were from the Palmach—Allon, Ratner, and Sadeh. The Commander of the Southern Front, which was composed of three Palmach battalions, was Brig.-General Yigal Allon, and one division was headed by a Palmach officer, Colonel S. Avidan. Out of some forty-five colonels at that time, twenty were Palmach officers. Between major and lieutenant-colonel, over 40% were Palmach officers. The commander of the officers' school was from the Palmach, as was his deputy and several of its senior instructors. The Army's Commander-in-Chief during the Six Days' War, Maj.-General Yitzhak Rabin, was Palmach headquarters operations chief in the Negev Campaign of 1948.

Since 1948, three Palmach officers have become Commander-in-Chief—Maj.-General Moshe Dayan (1953–1957), Yitzhak Rabin (1963–1967), and Chaim Bar-Lev (1968–)—and there have been at least forty brigadier-generals in the Israel Defence Army who were former Palmach officers. Three members of the present Israeli cabinet are former Palmach commanders: General Dayan, who is Minister of Defence, and General Allon, who is Minister of Labour. The Minister of Transportation, Moshe Carmel, is a former Palmach colonel, and Israel Galeeli, one of Palmach's founders and a former Chief of Staff of

Haganah, was Deputy Minister of Defence in 1948, and after the 1965 elections became Minister of Information.

"The Palmach", writes Israel Galeeli, "was in the kibbutz of the settlement movement"; the first unit of Haganah composed of Jews born in Palestine, its members "were followers of the doctrines of Pioneer Zionism—simple, monolithic, and strong."[8] This second generation entered Palestinian and Israeli politics from the Palmach, the military outlet for the rebels and anti-collaborationists who felt at home in the militant left wing of the HOL. The political and financial support of the Palmach came mainly from the kibbutz movement, which carried the heavy burden of maintaining the Palmach trainees in its settlements. Although Haganah contributed to Palmach's maintenance, it was apparent that Ben Gurion, who emerged as the leader of Haganah, by virtue of his growing responsibilities as the chief spokesman for a Jewish state and opposed factionalism, supported the Palmach reluctantly.

The Palmach ideology, which was impressed on volunteers in its training programmes and which was subsequently bequeathed to the Israel Defence Army, could be summarized as follows: (a) pride in the nation; (b) devotion to the principles of socialism and the kibbutz movement; (c) self-discipline; (d) egalitarianism; (e) leadership training; and (f) intellectual pursuits and culture.

Training for leadership was emphasized above all, and since the Palmach played a key role in determining the sort of leadership training offered by Haganah and later by the Israel Defence Army, this concept of leadership requires some elaboration.

The leadership and cadre programme of the Palmach was designed to produce not only professional but institutional leaders, men who were trained disseminators of Socialist-Zionist ideology. It aimed to achieve maximum quality in the officer. In some ways, and especially regarding its emphasis on cadre-building, the Palmach's leadership training recalls Lenin's ideas on revolutionary leadership. The principles of leadership developed by Yitzhak Dubnow,[9] Palmach's first professional commander of officer training, placed great emphasis on the role of the lowest ranking officer, the *mem-mem* (platoon leader). The mem-mem was earmarked for the most intensive training because he was the only commander who "has direct relations with his soldiers, and this direct contact is of utmost importance in the process of the creation of the lohem (the fighter)".

Leadership programmes also laid less emphasis on punishment as a system for disciplining the cadres. The mem-mem was to be exemplary, always able to withstand the hardest of conditions and serve as an inspiration to his men. Yet discipline could not be surrendered to volunteerism; the two were to be integrated in the mem-mem. "Our war machine", writes Dubnow, "must combine freedom and responsibility, discipline and laxity. The leader must be the link between the two. His functions must go beyond mastering technical skills, though he must be dedicated to essential military and professional ethics and standards."

Although the mem-mem course was the highest level of training offered up to 1948, the Israel Defence Army's present senior officers had little difficulty adjusting to higher command posts, so intensive was the training they received. Today, despite the existence of a large-scale army which demands higher as well as more complex and specialized forms of training, the mem-mem course remains basic and leadership is still inculcated as the primary responsibility of the commander.

Since the Palmach numbered no more than 1,300 men in 1941, when Nazi armies were marching toward Egypt and the Middle East, its morale and leadership training was geared to the waging of indirect, short-range guerrilla warfare.[10] The mobility of the unit and its divisibility into smaller units, sometimes composed of only two or three men, demanded great self-discipline, flexibility, courage, and the ability to make quick, on-the-spot decisions.

The Palmach was based in the kibbutzim under a two-year training-and-work programme, with most of the training shielded by the kibbutz. This integration of military functions and structural social formations contributed to the development of a high *esprit de corps* in the Palmach. The Palmach was thus to become the élite of the UKM, its political reservoir and an instrument for institutionalizing the kibbutz's domination over the HOL, the Yishuv, and its security instruments.

According to General Allon, Palmach's main sources of recruitment were: (1) the Agricultural Workers' Settlement, led by the kibbutz movement (UKM and the leftist national kibbutz) which, in co-ordination with the central (Haganah) recruitment agencies, supplied regular quotas for Palmach; (2) the old agricultural settlements (private enterprise) also bestowed some of their best sons to the Palmach; (3) a constant and encouraging source of recruitment were the Socialist youth movements (mainly based in the cities), as well as the Gadna (a Haganah youth group for ages 13–18 in the cities); (4) sporadic recruitment came from men who transferred out of Haganah's city forces.[11] See Table 2 for Bauer's estimate of the composition of the Palmach in June 1942, a year after its formation.[12]

Out of twenty-eight settlements which served as Palmach bases, seventeen belonged to UKM.[13] Through its growth in 1941–1947, UKM members in Palmach never dropped to less than 30%.[14] Out of 6 battalions, 4 battalions (1, 2, 3, and 5) were exclusively composed of recruits from agricultural settlements.

With the UKM militant, Sadeh, as its commanding officer and Israeli-born UKM member Allon as his deputy, it was only natural that the kibbutz movements and especially UKM

TABLE 2

Palmach Member Political Affiliation

Kibbutz Movement	Collectives	Cities	Private Agricultural Settlements
Ha-Kibbutz ha-Meuchad (United Kibbutz), affiliated with United Labour Party	350	41	
Hashomer Hatzair (National Kibbutz), affiliated with Mapam	200	24	
Ihud Ha-Kibbutzim (Kibbutz Federation), affiliated with Mapai	70	5	
No division by affiliation			250
TOTAL	620	70	940

should dictate much of the general staff policy, indoctrination, training, and ideology of the Palmach. Not only did the UKM prevail among Palmach's headquarters staff and its battalion commanders, but it also entrenched itself by means of its material and financial support. When the Palmach found itself in financial difficulties in early 1942 due to meagre Haganah support (out of Haganah's total budget of £230,000, Palmach was alloted only £23,000, and in July received only an additional £7,400),[15] the UKM Executive Committee stepped in offering the kibbutzim as training grounds. Taking all this into consideration, it is little wonder that the UKM viewed the Palmach as its prodigy. This relationship became something of a political problem in 1948 when the Palmach, under General Allon, in combination with other Israeli forces defeated the invading Eyptian army during the War of Liberation.

The NMO—Its Internal Organization and Ideology

The Bourgeois Zionists and farmers' associations played a key role in forming the Zionist-Revisionist group in Palestine which in turn objected strongly to Haganah's "takeover" by the Socialist left. Since the impact of the Revisionists on the Israel Defence Army is of marginal importance, attention will be paid only to the NMO's military underground apparatus, its internal organization, and sources of recruitment, and ideology—all of which are entirely unlike comparable structures of Haganah.[16]

The Fifth Immigration wave was a reservoir for Zionist-Revisionists as well as for its military groups. On the whole it consisted of Eastern European middle classes, primarily from Poland, who settled in urban areas and played a key role in the growth of Israel's urban centre, Tel-Aviv.[17]

The ideological divisions within the World Zionist movement had their impact on the Yishuv and its institutions. Jabotinsky, clearly the most powerful and charismatic leader of Zionist-Revisionism, was concerned about the intensification of Jewish political and military activities in Palestine. Jabotinsky challenged the World Zionist leadership for not acting effectively on such matters as anti-Semitism and Jewish assimilation. In Palestine, over the years 1920–1940, Jabotinsky went the full spectrum from encouraging co-operation with the Mandatory during the period of the Jewish Legions, 1916–1919, to advocating the transfer of the Palestine Mandate to more "responsible" powers (since the Passfield White Paper of 1930).[18]

Jabotinsky was away from Palestine for several years travelling abroad on behalf of Revisionist-Zionism. In his absence the Revisionist youth movement, Beitar, turned to active militarism, which he failed to harness on his return. Thus, although Jabotinsky himself never advocated total separation from London, his disciples, especially the young rebels, adopted total struggle against the Mandatory as their chief ideological goal. Not unlike Hehalutz, Beitar filled its ranks with youth from Eastern Europe. In Palestine, its major source of members was the Jewish middle-class sport movement, the Makabi. It also managed to attract a few extreme nationalist intellectuals of the Society for the Protection and Emulation of Hebrew which was active at Hebrew University. The Jewish Legions were the model for this youth movement which was distinguished (from Palmach) by its emphasis on strict military discipline, on ceremony, on uniforms, and epaulets.

Early in 1931 a group within Haganah began to protest against Histadrut's domination and urged more military action and less political involvement for Haganah. This group, led by Avraham Tehomi, wanted to see Haganah function as a professional military unit (along the lines of Jabotinsky's legion) without interference from the Yishuv's political parties. After a period of tension and conflict, the group captured a Haganah weapons arsenal in Jerusalem and formed a new and independent military unit called Haganah B.

In 1938 most of this group (some had returned to Haganah) joined with Beitar to form a new organization, NMO,[19] based on Jabotinsky's non-political professional soldier model. The NMO recruited members from among Beitar pioneers in Galilee and the old private agricultural settlements, Rosh-Pina, Kfar-Saba, Petah-Tiqvah, Rehovot Gedera, Rishon-Le-Zion, etc.[20] Thus the capitalist agricultural system, next to Tel-Aviv, became a major source of manpower for the NMO.

The ideological division between the two military structures could be described simply as "socialist" versus "capitalist" but that comparison is really not sufficient. The main difference between Haganah and the NMO revolved around the question of political commitment. Haganah B was formed because its founder objected to the "politicization" of Haganah by the Socialist left; they were striving toward a more "professional" army, and they joined with Beitar to form the NMO in pursuit of that same objective. However, the more the NMO acted as a free agent, independent of Beitar or Revisionist leadership, the more political it became, eventually forcing political decisions based on its military actions. In Haganah the reverse was true; it remained within the Socialist-Zionist framework and took its orders from the Yishuv. Its military actions were always dictated by the Yishuv's political decisions. Thus it is somewhat ironic that those who joined the NMO because they favoured a "professional" army actually encountered just the opposite. It was Haganah which was actually the more "professional" of the two, especially so *because* of its formal and informal domination by the Yishuv and its majority party.

The tension between the two erupted in a miniature Jewish civil war early in the 1940s. If it were not for the premature collapse of Stern's NMO group and the responsible action of Zionist Revisionists and Haganah leaders between 1939 and 1945, a major civil war would have taken place. NMO split several times and, by 1942, there were at least three factions in operation: Haganah B, NMO, and Lehi.

The weakness of NMO stemmed from two structural failures: one organizational and the other politico-ideological. The Farmers' Association, the Bourgeois Zionist and Zionist-Revisionist parties failed to dominate or manipulate the NMO. While Histadrut, Mapai, and Haganah were infiltrated, and the latter even dominated, by UKM and the agricultural kibbutz system, these in return *fully* and *thoroughly* accepted the final authority of the Jewish Agency and the Haganah. The Revisionist and Bourgeois Zionists failed to establish the mobilization structures that the Socialist-Zionists did. At best, they could protect or advise the NMO and its splinter groups but never dominate or harness that group. The organizational objectives of the Farmers' Association were limited. It was not a political organization as was the Histadrut. It was institutionally limited to economic functions, such as co-operation in supplies, marketing, and credit. Its function was particularistic, and although it espoused universal and political interests, the organization was not structured and mobilized for these purposes.[21] In fact, the Farmers' Association "strongly opposed the policies of the country-wide political institutions such as the Jewish Agency or the underground military organization (the Haganah) whenever these ignored economic or local interests".[22]

The greatest weakness of the Revisionists and NMO was ideological. While Labour Zionists were veterans of World Socialist and Revolutionary movements, Jabotinsky, although one of Zionism's most talented leaders, was not a great ideological innovator. A journalist, an orator, and a brilliant propagandist, he was best suited to practical and mass politics. Thus his movement inherited zeal, activism, and pragmatism from its founder but no organizational and ideological heritage equal to that of the Socialist-Zionists. Jabotinsky, the heroic nationalist, was a symbol for Beitar and NMO, but as a political tactician he actually failed the movement.

Jabotinsky ignored the Arab community in Palestine and this disposition also left its impact on the NMO. Avraham Stern's group advocated only one goal—the ousting of the foreign powers from Palestine—and developed virtually no policy toward the Arabs.

Revisionist and Socialist ideologies were furthest apart on the subject of the Jewish community's political future in Palestine. The Socialist-Zionists envisioned a democratic Socialist Jewish commonwealth with a co-operative-based economy. The Revisionists, on the other hand, encouraged the development of a democratic bourgeoise society tied to a capitalist system of free enterprise.

In a mission-orientated community the Revisionists and the NMO had little success in attracting the volunteer-minded youth in the agricultural collective settlements who were more or less at the disposal of the HOL. In the cities also the competition favoured the HOL with its powerful trade union movement and their youth movement outnumbered Beitar. When Stern's group found itself short on finances and resorted to terrorism and robbery, they alienated in the process one of their few potential reservoirs, the private agricultural sector of the population.

An additional blow to Revisionism and the NMO was the death of three of their most effective leaders in the short space of two years, 1940–1942. Jabotinsky died in 1940; Raziel in 1941;

TABLE 3

Control over Headquarters of Haganah

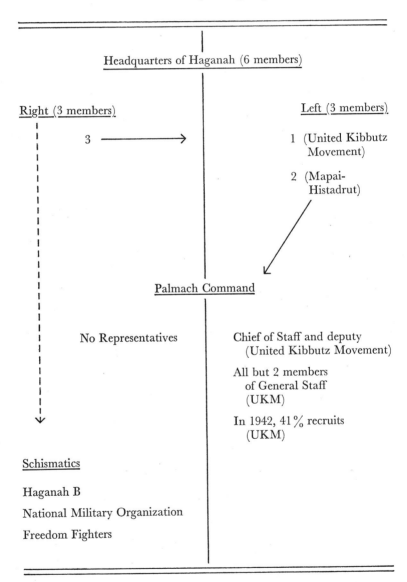

Headquarters of Haganah (6 members)

Right (3 members)

3 ⟶

Left (3 members)

1 (United Kibbutz
Movement)

2 (Mapai-
Histadrut)

Palmach Command

No Representatives

Chief of Staff and deputy
(United Kibbutz Movement)

All but 2 members
of General Staff
(UKM)

In 1942, 41% recruits
(UKM)

Schismatics

Haganah B

National Military Organization

Freedom Fighters

and Stern in 1942. Deprived of a charismatic personality around which to mobilize, the NMO in its third incarnation, the Lehi (Freedom Fighters of Israel), devoted all its energy to terrorist activities against the British in Palestine. After the White Paper proclamation early in 1939, NMO could still attract the attention of the Yishuv. But when some of the NMO's later terrorist activities ended in destruction of Jewish life and property,[23] it became known as the Gangster-Terrorist group and lost its appeal to the Yishuv—bitter as the Yishuv was about the Mandatory. Stern's and Lehi's attempts to collaborate with the Fascists and Nazis in Eastern Europe, during World War II, only brought more degradation upon this movement.[24] The call to oust the British was lost in the Nazi horror but the NMO re-emerged after 1945 under the leadership of Menahem Begin.

NOTES

1. Dinour, *History of Haganah, op. cit.*, Vol. I, Part II, p. 942.
2. On Wingate see Christopher Sykes, *Orde Wingate* (Cleveland, Ohio: World Publishers, 1959).
3. *Ibid.*, p. 225. Also Bauer, *Diplomatia Ve-Mahteret (Diplomacy and Underground in Zionism 1939–1945)* (Heb.) (Merhavia: Sifriat Poalim, 1966), pp. 97–98; Dinour, *History of Haganah, op. cit.*, Vol. II, Part II, pp. 911–13
4. General Yigal Allon, "Deeds and Determination", in Zrubavel Gilad (ed.), *Sepher Ha-Palmach (The Book of Palmach)* (Heb.) (2 vols.), Vol. I (Tel-Aviv: Ha-Kibbutz ha-Meuchad, 1955), pp. 248–49.
5. Dinour, *History of Haganah, op. cit.*, Vol. II, Part II, pp. 1014–15.
6. Bauer, *Diplomacy, op. cit.*, p. 18.
7. Hurewitz, *The Struggle, op. cit.*, pp. 134–45.
8. Israel Galeeli, "The Palmach—A Seed of the Labor Movement", in Zvi Ra'anan (ed.), *Zava U-Milhama (Army and War in Israel and among Nations)* (Heb.) (Tel-Aviv: Sifriat Poalim, 1955), p. 763.
9. Y. Dubnow in *Book of Palmach, op. cit.*, Vol. I.
10. Bauer, *Diplomacy, op. cit.*
11. Yigal Allon, *The Palmach, op. cit.*, pp. 31–34.
12. Bauer, *Diplomacy, op. cit.*, pp. 160–61.
13. *Ibid.*, p. 161.
14. Weintraub, *Chequered Cloth*, MS. p. 333.
15. Bauer, *Diplomacy, op. cit.*, p. 139.
16. For the history of Revisionist military organizations, see Dinour, *History of Haganah, op. cit.*, and Niv, *Battle for Freedom, op. cit.*
17. Dinour, *History of Haganah*, Vol. II, Part I, p. 481. About 80% of this immigration settled in urban areas.
18. On Jabotinsky see Schechtman, *Rebel, op. cit.*
19. For the story of NMO by its official historian, see Niv, *Battle for Freedom, op. cit.*, Vol. I, pp. 156–77. The Haganah's point of view is found in Dinour, *History of Haganah, op. cit.*, Vol. II, Part I, pp. 574–85, and Vol. II, Part II, pp. 1053–72.

20. Niv, *Battle for Freedom, op. cit.*, pp. 228–35.

21. For an excellent analysis of the Farmers' Association's institutional goals see Weintraub, *Chequered Cloth, op. cit.*, MS. pp. 70–97, 478–85.

22. *Ibid.*, p. 481.

23. Niv, *Battle for Freedom, op. cit.*, pp. 279–302; and Dinour, *History of Haganah, op. cit.*, Vol. II, Part II, pp. 1053–72.

24. Dinour, *ibid.*, pp. 1066–67; Niv, *Battle for Freedom, op. cit.*, Vol. I, pp. 300–01. Niv naturally does not admit the open Jabotinsky–Stern split.

Part Two

The Army of Israel

CHAPTER IV

The Era of Transition

As World War II drew to a close, the drive to create an independent Jewish state escalated. It had become clear to the Jews that Britain could not uphold the Mandate, nor would it participate in the creation of a Jewish state.[1] Accordingly, the Jewish Agency, acting in the capacity of a shadow government, began to intensify its efforts in the following directions:

1. Organizing the exodus of Jewish refugees from Europe to Palestine.

2. Alerting world public opinion, especially in America, to the plight of the Jews and the urgent need to establish a Jewish state.

3. Mobilizing the Yishuv for a possible military confrontation with the Arabs.

Military mobilization and the great exodus from Europe were related. A shortage of men and resources forced the Yishuv to determine priorities and, up to 1947, the salvation of the Jewish refugees came first. Thus Ha-'Apala (the organization resonsible for the exodus) consumed the best men and most of the money while Haganah received meagre allotments by comparison.[2] It was not until the struggle for Palestine had commenced in earnest that maximum efforts were expended in both directions.

The Mobilization of Men and Resources

In 1946 the budget of the Haganah was less than £400,000. The total membership of Haganah was around 45,000 or just 7% of the population of the Yishuv.[3] Haganah field units (Hish) had only 700 trained officers, responsible for 7,000 men—all of whom were part-time volunteers. The Youth Brigades—numbering approximately 10,000—did not amount to much more than a reservoir for the armed forces, since their members were still in school or under the age of 18. The Palmach numbering around 2,000 was the only full-time professional force ready for combat.

To alleviate the shortages of men and finances, Haganah was forced to take the initiative and launched a large-scale fund drive in Palestine (Kofer Ha-Yeshuv or Community Chest) and among world Jewry, especially in the United States.[4] It also began a widespread campaign to recruit new members. Here the problem was acute, for Haganah drew upon the same pool of "professional" nation-builders as did Hityashvut and Histadrut. Another problem was the fact that the majority of the urban community (over 50%)[5] was not as concerned as the agricultural settlement system with security matters. Histadrut and the workers' councils in Tel-Aviv, Haifa, and Jerusalem neglected the Haganah and concentrated their attention on social welfare and health activities. The clash between the Revisionists and Socialist-Zionists slowed the increase of Haganah manpower and the fear of a leftist takeover of the Haganah discouraged several dedicated and organizationally talented leaders of the right from joining.[6]

In June 1947 Ben Gurion, the head of the Jewish Agency, took over the defence portfolio. He set out to accomplish two tasks: (1) the reorganization of Haganah, to make it responsible *only* to national authorities; and (2) the rapid and intensive mobilization of men and resources, so that Yishuv would have an army ready to meet the expected Arab invasion.

By October 1947, only six months after Ben Gurion had taken charge of defence matters, Haganah's budget had risen to £3·3 million,[7] the highest in Haganah history. Under his direction the Palmach was strengthened and enlarged; the scope of Haganah's purchasing operation in Europe was widened; a group of former Jewish partisans was organized in France; Jewish volunteers were recruited in the United States; the Jewish Brigade and Haganah were mobilized to bring trained men and volunteers to Palestine; and all the financial resources, of World Zionism were invested in the task of arming and training an independent Jewish military force in Palestine. Thus on May 1948 the United Nations assigned date for British departure from Palestine, Ben Gurion had an army ready to command.

In order to accomplish the above, Ben Gurion had to unify

the autonomous and semi-autonomous military structures which had previously been responsible for those functions. The task was monumental but he proved equal to it. He moved toward unification in stages, gradually achieving his objective by transferring all military functions to the Provisional Government under his authority. In the process, he abolished Haganah's headquarters, its general staff, and the parity system by which promotions were determined. The rivalries between the various military organizations in Palestine complicated his task and he found opposition coming from all directions. The NMO refused to accept the authority of the Provisional Government and the Palmach persisted in operating its own general staff, even though it acknowledged the authority of the Provisional Government and its defence minister.

Conflict and Co-operation between Military Structures

The relationship between Haganah and the NMO illustrates the organizational, ideological, and political chasm which divided Zionism's left and right movements. The HOL-Haganah and Revisionist-NMO converged only on one point—the realization that a Jewish army could play a significant role in determining political independence in Palestine and the type of social system to be established thereafter. The political and socio-ideological polarity between Haganah–Palmach and the NMO could not have been wider and the various attempts to bridge the two ended in failure.[8] For the sake of continuing the struggle against the Mandatory and for the sake of preserving their organizations, however, Haganah and the NMO postponed a showdown and some measure of co-operation was established between them prior to independence. Had they not co-operated, they would have destroyed each other which almost certainly would have doomed Israel's political future.

Ben Gurion, the chairman of the Jewish Agency, opposed co-operation and united action between Haganah and the NMO, especially after the NMO's resort to terrorism, even though Golomb, Galeeli, and other Haganah leaders sought reconciliation with NMO splinter groups. An attempt to create a military superstructure, Am-Lohem (fighting nation), encompassing both never got off the ground since it was the Revisionist leaders who initiated the move.[9]

E

In 1944, for a very brief period, the three—Haganah, NMO, Lehi—co-ordinated military action without Ben Gurion's approval. Toward the close of the war, however, the Jewish Agency was preparing itself for the diplomatic moves that were to help create an independent Jewish state and Ben Gurion and other Agency leaders felt that co-operation with the "terrorists" would burden the Jewish cause. Thus Haganah was instructed to co-operate with British intelligence authorities by informing on the NMO. This was the notorious Sezon era. Not all of the Haganah command co-operated nor did the UKM leadership, who refused to inform on fellow Jews. The UKM left its Palmach members free, however, to decide individually whether or not to implement the Yishuv's order. In the end, the moderates prevailed and United Labour and Palmach were both instrumental in bringing the Sezon affair to a close in 1945.[10]

On May 31, 1948, Zahal was officially proclaimed as the army of Israel, and the war against the Arabs temporarily blurred the political conflicts which smouldered beneath the surface. The Palmach became Zahal's élite force and was organized into the army which led Israeli forces to victory against the Egyptians in the Negev. The Commander of the Southern Front, Brig.-General Allon, was the Palmach's chief. By organizing Palmach's battalions under his command, Allon, a brilliant organizational and military tactician, turned a victory against Egypt into a political challenge to Ben Gurion. The challenge was serious, since Palmach with its brilliant commanders and victorious forces—acting under the authority of the Defence Minister and in unison with Zahal's General Staff—emerged as an autonomous military organization taking credit for defeating Israel's most formidable rival. But Ben Gurion was not be undermined. On October 29, 1948, Zahal's Chief of Staff, Maj.-General Ya'aqov Dori, following the direction of Ben Gurion, ordered that Palmach headquarters be dissolved by November 7, 1948, and that Allon henceforth serve only in the capacity of Southern Front Commander.

The NMO had been dissolved earlier, following a showdown late in June 1948, in Tel-Aviv and Natanya. Ben Gurion ordered a Palmach battalion stationed in Tel-Aviv to destroy the *Altalena*, a ship commanded by the NMO, which was attempting to unload arms to its troops waiting on the shores of Natanya along the Mediterranean coast, between Haifa and Tel-Aviv. Had this confrontation resulted in civil war, it would have curtailed the immense defence effort necessary to win against the Arabs. The NMO and Menahem Begin, facing some opposition from other NMO leaders, played a key role in bringing about the final acceptance by the NMO of the national authority of the Jewish Agency.[11]

NOTES

1. See Ben Gurion, *Ba-Ma'aracha (In the Battle)* (Heb.), Vol. V (Tel-Aviv: Ayanot, 1947–1955), pp. 135–37; and also Ben Gurion's Preface to the *History of the War of Liberation, op. cit.*, pp. 25–27.

2. The most definitive history of Ha-'Apala and the exodus will be found in three forthcoming volumes on the *History of the Haganah* which the author read in galley form in October 1967 in Tel-Aviv. For a discussion of the role played by the Palmach's special branch, the Palyam (naval Shock Platoons), see Allon, *Palmach, op. cit.*, pp. 155–79.

3. Ben Gurion, Preface, *op. cit.*, pp. 26, 28; Ben Gurion, "From the Diary: April–May 1948", *Ma-Ariv* (April 30, 1968), p. 25, listed the existing number of Haganah men and equipment.

4. Ben Gurion, Preface, *op. cit.*, pp. 26–28.

5. For statistics on membership see Dinour, *History of Haganah, op. cit.*, Vol. II, Part II, pp. 1003–13; also see *Statistical Handbook Jewish Agency for Palestine* (1949), pp. 47–48.

6. Out of a population of 400,000 Jews in Palestine, only 30,000 (less than 10%, not counting 5,500 women) were registered Haganah members and of these only 3,000–4,000 were employed fulltime. See Dinour, *History of Haganah, op. cit.*, Vol. II, Part III (1964), Table 7, p. 1392.

7. *Ibid.*, p. 44.

8. Bauer, *Diplomacy, op. cit.*, pp. 265–83.

9. *Ibid.*, pp. 267–69.

10. *Ibid.*, p. 281. The symposium held on Sezon by *Ma-Ariv*.

11. Recent literature, especially the proliferating memorabilia on the pre-1948 defence and military organization and exploits, modifies the actual threat presented by *Altalena*. See Eliahu Lankin, *The Story of Altalena* (Heb.) (Tel-Aviv: Hadar, 1967). General Yigael Yadin considered the fall of the old city of Jerusalem and other failures caused by the lack of military united command and by NMO activities independent from Palmach and Haganah in 1948 in Jerusalem. See "The War of Independence", interview in *Ma-Ariv*, May 14, 1967, pp. 9–11.

CHAPTER V

Civil–Military Relations:
The Israeli Formula

THE transformation of Israel's voluntary, semi-professional, and highly politicized security organizations into a unified, compulsory, professional, and depoliticized army was accomplished by the determination and skill of David Ben Gurion. As Premier and Defence Minister from 1947 to 1963 (interrupted for 15 months between 1953 and 1955), Ben Gurion stamped his indelible mark on Israel's army and Defence Ministry. More than any other factors, his personality and nationalist vision shaped the course of civil–military relations in the new state of Israel.

In April 1948, the Provisional Government's defence portfolio was formally instituted as the Ministry of Defence in the government of Israel. In assuming responsibility for defence, Ben Gurion recalls that "I made it clear to the Provisional Government when it delegated the defence portfolio to me . . . that I would accept the ministry only under the following conditions: (1) The army that will be formed [Zahal] and all its branches be subordinated to the government of the people and only to *that* government. (2) All persons acting on behalf of the army or the Haganah will act only according to a clearly defined function established by the government of the people. The procedures which prevailed in the Haganah could not and will not prevail when the army of the state of Israel will be established."[1]

The following are the unwritten but firmly institutionalized concepts and procedures initiated by the first defence minister of Israel:

1. The nationalization, formalization, and depoliticization of the army.

2. The supremacy of civilian authorities in determining the issues of war and peace in Israel.

3. The defence minister as the final arbiter of conflicts between civilians and the military.

4. The direct and permanent control of the defence minister over the integrity, the morale, and the professional standards of the officer corps.

5. A highly centralized decision-making process in matters of defence and related foreign policy issues limited to a small and highly cohesive group of civilian and military selected and dominated by the defence minister.

As Defence Minister, Ben Gurion set out to accomplish the following: (1) To consolidate all offices and functions related to security held previously by independent or autonomous political or military structures by centralizing authority in his hands. (2) To define and separate the functions of chief of staff and "head of war" previously fused in the office of the head of Haganah.

At the helm of the Defence Ministry, Ben Gurion assumed the policy-making function of "head of war" while Zahal's chief of staff was delegated the operational function of maintaining and training the army—the instrument of war. The chief of staff, although clearly subordinate to the defence minister, was allowed considerable independence and autonomy on purely military matters. A parallel office of director general was created in the Defence Ministry to administer the support function of supplying and arming the military. The director general was independent of the army and directly subordinate to the defence minister. The appointment of Zahal's chief of staff and the director general of the Ministry was ultimately the responsibility of the defence minister.

Although the formal organization of the defence establishment determined the basic operational ground rules, personalities played at least an equal role in influencing the development of institutional practices and procedures.

Having assumed the position of head of war, Ben Gurion created an *ad hoc* kitchen cabinet to advise him, which was composed of one or two favourite cabinet members, Mapai's "army specialists", several senior civil servants, Zahal's chief of staff, the chief of intelligence, and a few selected senior officers and personal advisers. The members of the group met only at Ben Gurion's request and their individual or collective influence varied according to circumstances and force of personality; unswerving loyalty to Ben Gurion was the common bond between them. The group advised not only on questions of military strategy and doctrine but on foreign policy issues as well. This *ad-hoc* cabinet was vested with responsibility for making major decisions concerning Israel's security and the army's future. Cabinet ministers, while exempted from the actual decision-making process, were nevertheless expected to approve and defend these policies at home and abroad.

Among those around Ben Gurion were Shaul Avigor, the former Head of Haganah, Iser Arel, the Chief of Intelligence and Espionage, *Ha-Mosad* (not to be confused with Zahal's Intelligence Division, *Aman*), and other *ad hoc* "security experts".

The type of authority which Ben Gurion exercised in relation to his subordinates would be defined by Weber as charismatic authority. Weber's biographer, Bendix, has characterized this as "domination on the basis of leadership, the extraordinary power of a person and the identification of followers with that person".[2] Such authority is legitimatized by the creation of disciples which is not easy to do, especially in a democratic society like Israel. But two disciples emerged and became dominant figures in their own right. They were General Moshe Dayan, Zahal's Chief of Staff from 1953 to 1957, and Shimon Peres, who was Director General from 1953 to 1959 and Deputy Defence Minister from 1959 to 1965.

In prestige and importance, the Defence Ministry has always ranked second to Zahal. The army fell heir to the reputation and role of its predecessor, Haganah, while the Defence Ministry was relegated to the unglamorous task of quarter-mastership. Zahal officers have traditionally regarded the Ministry as a cluster of "clerks and merchants".

While Zahal received the best of intellectual and organizational attention, the Ministry of Defence was neglected. In its early days, the Ministry was run by prominent politicians and technocrats such as Levi Eshkol (its first Director General and now the Prime Minister), Pinhas Sapir (its second Director General, formerly Minister of Finance and now Secretary

General of Israel Labour Party, M'ai), Israel Galeeli (First Deputy Minister of Defence, now Minister of Information), Shaul Avigor (Head of Haganah), and others. When it became apparent to these politicians that the Defence Ministry was dominated by Ben Gurion, they saw little opportunity to further their own ambitions and left. Galeeli was phased out, but continued to serve occasionally on an *ad hoc* basis, over a dispute with Ben Gurion on the relationships between the minister and Zahal. According to Ben Gurion, Galeeli agreed with him that the Palmach headquarters should be abolished and that its battalions could be directly under the chief command (Zahal's general staff), but that he, Galeeli, would be the *intermediary* between the defence minister (Ben Gurion) and Zahal's chief of staff. In the end Ben Gurion prevailed and Galeeli did resign; and the office of Head of Haganah was finally abolished by Ben Gurion.[3]

Although Ben Gurion is frequently given credit for having strengthened the civilian arm of defence, he actually boosted the role of Zahal as against the Ministry. As Minister of Defence, he institutionzlied the primacy of the army in the Ministry, primarily for personal and political reasons. He established a special type of relationship with the army's high command and during Dayan's tenure as Chief of Staff was on especially close terms with the senior officers who were moulded in the Ben Gurion–Dayan image. In contrast to his intense interest in military affairs, Ben Gurion generally left the administration of the Defence Ministry to its directors except where high-level political decisions were involved.

Officially, the army was responsible to the government of Israel—a coalition composed of Mapai and the small Socialist, religious, and liberal parties. In reality, however, neither Mapai nor Mapai ministers in the cabinet had very much influence over the army. The smaller parties in the coalition were rarely consulted on army or defence matters. The Knesset's Defence and Foreign Affairs Committee was docile and *pro-forma* group. From outside the government, the United Labour Party still exercised some influence on military decisions because of its strong historical involvement with defence. Galeeli, Allon, and former Palmach commanders were consulted on defence matters, but beyond this their influence declined. The kibbutz movement still conducted defence seminars (organized by former Palmach officers) and offered criticism, but to little effect.

For all practical purposes, the army fell solely under the jurisdiction of Ben Gurion in his dual role of Prime Minister and Minister of Defence. He exercised control over the defence establishment by assuming the responsibility for making the final decision on foreign policy matters relating to war and peace and by his power to appoint and promote top-level army officers. In this sense, he acted more as supreme commander than as defence minister.

Ben Gurion viewed Israel as a state with its back to the sea, surrounded by hostile Arab governments. In these circumstances, the fate of the nation rested on the ability of the army to defend it and the political wisdom of the man responsible for the conduct of foreign policy.

In order to keep the army from engaging in party politics and to make Zahal more professional, Ben Gurion assumed power to approve all appointments and promotions from chief of staff down to lieutenant-colonel. The outgoing chief of staff had considerable influence on the choice of a successor. Before acting on his recommendation, however, Ben Gurion usually consulted some of his chief informal advisers. When it came to determining the appointment or promotion of other senior officers, Ben Gurion relied heavily on the recommendations of the chief of staff and members of the high command, and he and Dayan worked especially well together for Dayan was a loyal Ben Gurionite, dedicated to the same principles as his chief.[4] In this way Ben Gurion did leave the high command considerable political leverage over security and promotions policy. However, throughout Ben Gurion's tenure the high command never approximated that of Moltke's.[5] In fact, the relationships between Lavon and the high command were more reminiscent of the French experience especially during the Dreyfus period.[6]

Ben Gurion used his appointive powers to assure that the army maintained a youthful leadership. He believed that an army composed mainly of reserves should be geared to handle rapid shifts in rank to allow for the emergence of new talent.[7] As this would suggest, promotions at levels below the high command were based primarily on merit and, on the whole, a suitably apolitical and professional atmosphere was maintained. As will be shown, however, not even Ben Gurion's considerable efforts could entirely prevent a powerful army high command system from intervening in politics.

Under General Dayan, the powers and prestige of Zahal's chief of staff and the high command far outweighed those of the director general of the Ministry. This did not occur because of strong personalities in Zahal and weak ones in the Defence Ministry, nor because of Ben Gurion's propensity to favour the army over the Ministry. It resulted from Zahal's superior prestige, cohesion, and purpose. The Defence Ministry was a relative newcomer which had not yet distinguished itself nor could it share with Zahal the credit for liberating the nation in 1948.

The army was actually the first bureaucratic structure to be successfully transformed from an autonomous pre-independence organization into a truly national institution subordinate to the government. This was achieved by taking the army out of politics.

Ben Gurion banned political groups from operating actively within Zahal and replaced the political parity system with a merit system for determining appointments and promotions. His objective was clear: the removal of the left from the positions of influence they had secured in the defence establishment. In doing so, Ben Gurion frustrated the ambitions of many Palmach commanders and ideologues. They eventually made a mass exodus from the army and were followed by many ranking politicians who resigned from the Defence Ministry.

The problem was how to thwart the formation of a leftist people's army or the creation of a professional clique divorced from the nation and its ideals. Ben Gurion succeeded in averting these extremes by establishing an army whose ideological and moral values were democratic and egalitarian and not collectivist—a Socialist people's army—or professionalist, operating outside the context of Israel's goals and social values.

The dissolution of Palmach's general staff and the NMO was no small task. Throughout 1948–1949, a controversy raged in the councils of the HOL, in the cabinet, in Zahal's high command, and among the public over the future of Palmach in

Zahal. The question was also reflected in the parliamentary debates on the Defence Service Bill, the Veteran's Law, and the Military Jurisdiction Law.

Ben Gurion, supported by Avigor and Generals Dori (Zahal's first Chief of Staff), Yadin (its second Chief of Staff), advocated the creation of a professional regular army with a vast and permanent reserve system, while former Palmach commanders and ideologues, led by Sadeh, Allon, and Galeeli, promoted the formation of a people's army, very much like Palmach, based on small and highly mobile units, whose backbone remains the collective agricultural system, but especially maintaining the high command close to Palmach.

The transformation of Haganah into Zahal was made relatively easy because of the war. "Due to the urgent matters of war and the declaration of independence", writes Ben Gurion, "no final decision concerning the organization of Zahal took place in the meetings of the Provisional Government. . . . So the decision of the Provisional Government and the organization of Zahal [on the final authority of the defence minister in matters of defence] did not prevail due to the divisions within the military forces."[8] National unity against the Arab invaders prevailed over particular and politically interested groups.

The integration of the formerly autonomous military organizations into Zahal could have been accomplished only with their co-operation. Because Zahal's new general staff was a carry-over from Haganah's general staff, the co-operation between Palmach's Southern Command and Zahal's headquarters was understandably smooth. Generals Yadin and Laskov later testified to this in the midst of the Palmach challenge to Ben Gurion's leadership. The war eased the integration of autonomous military units by uniting them under one command. But the key to the accomplishment of this formidable task was the persistent, stubborn, and autocratic personality—Ben Gurion. From 1947 to his last day as Defence Minister in 1963, Zahal was his chief concern.

Ben Gurion's efforts to dissolve and remove the extra-political and ideological aspects inherited by Zahal from Haganah, Palmach, and the NMO, ran into formidable opposition. Even those officers who favoured depoliticization of the army were reluctant to abandon the Haganah and Palmach legacies. A group of Palmach officers, including their most prominent officer and former commander, Yigal Allon, resigned from the army as soon as the armistice with the Arabs at Rhodes (1949) was concluded.

These officers, on the whole, argued that the professionalization of the army and the "isolation" of its officer corps would undermine the pioneer-egalitarian spirit of the kibbutz and Palmach, and that it could also undermine the commitment to service of Israeli society. This group generally advocated extra-political functions for the army and especially for its officer corps. Ben Gurion and other senior officers strongly believed that the army's primary task was on the battlefield; they envisioned a small, but highly professional, army. Ben Gurion probably overreacted to the NMO and Palmach controversies, for in the end even he could not accept such a narrow role for the Israeli army.

It was hoped that dedication to professional skills in a stable society would decrease the extra-curricular and political activities of the professionals. And indeed, the functional proliferation of the Israeli army has not only reduced but, in some ways, extinguished the political concern in dedicated officers. The military was limited to its function—protecting the state from external aggression and war.

A comprehensive study of political articulation and commitment, and political interventionist tendencies (and we clearly separate the two) of Zahal's officer corps is not yet available. Political articulation is correlated to the educational level of the officers and Israeli officers born in the Arab countries with low education are low in political consciousness. The better trained and educated are politically articulate but also highly professional. Politically conscious to a high degree are young officers from the kibbutzim, especially from Mapam Socialist collectives.

On the whole, the social isolation (not to be confused with a societal isolation) of professional officers and their apolitical attitudes has been greater than among the Haganah–Palmach and the 1948–1950 Zahal officer corps. However, this type of corporate and professional separatism is the hallmark of the professional soldier. Because Zahal is a people's army and a reserve organization, its barracks life is short, the officers are permanently integrated with society, and the chances of officers becoming ideologically or professionally independent are minimal. In Israel, the chance of a particularly long military career is remote because the officer corps is continuously rotated and thus is kept young.

The kibbutzim encourage their young men to volunteer for training as pilots, paratroopers, or other élite military occupations. One of Ben Gurion's major efforts, after 1956, was to direct kibbutz-born inductees to join these élite corps; the experience of Sinai had proven to him that a high proportion of able and valiant leaders had come from the agrarian collective settlements.[9] This was reaffirmed in 1967. While the collective settlements are no more than 4% of Israel's population, 25% of the total killed and wounded Zahal officers were from the kibbutzim. (See Tables 4 and 5.)

The training of young officers (ages 17–19) emphasizes their role as leaders and socializers. The fraternity type and the small group are still the models for Israeli army units. Many of Palmach's leadership training principles have been included in the army's officer training programme and, as in the Palmach, the *mem-mem* (platoon leader) is to serve as a model for the new recruits, most of whom have immigrated to Israel since 1948. The career of a junior officer is totally dependent upon achievement, and leadership ability is the key to promotion. Only a small number of men elect the army as a career. After a few years' service, the junior officer is considered ready to pursue further education or to assume junior management positions in industry and government.

Prior to 1962 most senior officers had originally served in the Palmach, the Haganah, or the British army, but since then they have been joined by men who were junior officers during the Sinai Campaign (see Table 6).

The senior officers provided a valuable core of leadership in the early phases of political modernization but few, if any, leaders with political interventionist inclinations have emerged from the present senior officer group.

The most significant change in political institutions and practices in the new state was the growing formalization and bureaucratization: voluntary civil action gave way to formal compulsory service. The creation of Zahal from the Haganah

TABLE 4

*1963–1964 Conscripts: Rate of Basic Qualification
and Career Mobility in Percentages**

Rate of Basic Qualification	Sons of Kibbutzim	Others
1 (highest)	69	23
2	43	21
3	39	28
4	51	24
5	32	19
6	22	8
7 (lowest)	33	3

* Intelligence, education, knowledge of Hebrew, personal qualifications, and country of birth.
(Table 13, p. 258)

TABLE 5

*Fitness for Command Positions Among
Zahal's Conscripts in Percentages*

	1961–1962 Conscripts			1963–1964 Conscripts		
Fitness	Sons of Kibbutz	Educated in Kibbutz	Other	Sons of Kibbutz	Educated in Kibbutz	Other
High	60	50	46	65	52	54
Medium	21	20	31	12	22	14
Low	19	30	23	23	26	32

(Table 11, p. 257)
SOURCE: Y. Amir, "Sons of Kibbutzim in Zahal", *Megamot*, Vol. 15, Nos. 2–3 (August 1967).

illustrates how a colonizing movement and a society of social mission, predominantly maintained with primary, non-formalized groups, were transformed into formal bureaucratic structures.

S. N. Eisenstadt holds that "All this did not give rise to a pure Weberian type of neutral bureaucracy. The non-bureaucratic elements existed not only on the top, directive levels ... but became strongly interwoven also at other levels."[10] The organizatton of Zahal corroborates all aspects of this change:

TABLE 6   *Zahal's Senior Officers Affiliation with Defence Structures before 1948*

Prime Minister Name	Tenure	Minister of Defence Name	Tenure	Commander-in-Chief Name	Tenure	Affil.	B	H	P	ZG	Total Senior General Staff Officers
Ben Gurion	1948–Dec. 1953	Ben Gurion	1948–Dec. 1953	Dori	1948–1951	H	3	10	1		14
				Yadin		H					
				Makleff	1952–1953	B	5	5	2		12
				Dayan		P					
Sharett	Dec. 1953–Nov. 1955	Lavon	Dec. 1953–Feb. 1955	Dayan	1953–1955	P	4	6	1		11
Ben Gurion	Nov. 1955–Jun. 1963	Ben Gurion	Feb. 1955–Jun. 1963	Dayan	1955–1957	P	6	6	1		13
				Laskov			6	5	2		13
				Laskov	1957–58	B	6	4	3		13
				Laskov	1958–59		6	4	3		13
				Laskov	1959–1960	B	6	2	5		13
				Tsur	1960–61	H	4	3	6		13
				Tsur	1961–62	H	3	3	7		13
				Rabin	1962–63	P					
Eshkol	Jun. 1963–present	Eshkol	1963–Jun. 1967	Rabin	1963–65	P	4	3	8	Sharon	15
				Rabin	1965–66		1	5	11	Sharon	18
				Bar-Lev	1966–67		1	5	10	Sharon	17
		Dayan	Jun. 1967–present	Bar-Lev	1968–present	P	1	5	10	Sharon	17
Predicted			1968–1970			P	1	4	8	4	

Key: H—Haganah;   P—Palmach;   B—British Army;   ZG—Zahal Graduate.

* Of 52 senior officers, ranking lieutenant-colonel and above, 23 came from the British Army, 3 from the Palmach, the

from voluntary to compulsory social and political action; from non-formal to formal organization; and intervention of non-bureaucratic elements at all levels.

Formalization, bureaucratization, function differentiation, and economic modernization mitigated collective obligations, the co-operative enterprise, the egalitarian distribution of income and economic and social power. These changes in social structure and ideology were reflected in Zahal and increasingly made their impact upon the officer class. Economic modernization, political mobilization and formalization, functional specializations, social and status differentiation, all served to restrict the practices of recruitment and political mobilization which had been established by Haganah.

The process by which Yishuv institutions and structures were politically demobilized deserves attention both for historical and analytical reasons. Although this is not the place to deal with the subject in depth, it is noteworthy in view of Zahal's distinction as the first structure to be successfully institutionalized and bureaucratized.

In Israel, the demobilization of a number of institutions and structures was correlated with the dictates of political power. The power of most Yishuv organizations derived from the voluntary groups which supported them. The political task of the government, the bureaucracy and the army, therefore, was to nationalize and formalize these institutions, structures, and procedures.

To politically disarm these structures required, of course, a monumental effort. The philosophy inherent in the policies of the Yishuv and Socialist-Zionism was Revolutionary Constructivism—a doctrine of accumulating political, social, and economic power under the Mandatory—which led to the establishment of powerful and interested political and economic structures to fulfil their goals.

Zahal was the first to be nationalized and formalized. In fact, it was to become the model of a demobilized, institutional, and bureaucratic structure in Israel. Had the army remained politically autonomous—styling itself along the mobilizing principles of UKM—it would have become a political instrument of the small, but militant, pioneer élite based in the agricultural settlements and in the kibbutzim.[11]

And yet, the process of formalization in the army after the

integration of Palmach—NMO into Zahal could not proceed without the legacy of the past. The tasks of modernization, rapid integration of immigrants, and functional proliferation imposed upon Zahal a new role—the maker of citizens, the inculcator of civic and nationalist culture. Here the traditions of Haganah and Palmach were again of great service—not as a component for the accumulation of political, social, and economic power but as an instrument of the state advancing the aims of national integration, political mobilization, and economic modernization.

Ben Gurion established the HOL to strengthen the state, not particularist interests. He argued that the leadership of the HOL, caught up in its socialistic preconceptions, was arresting the processes of modernization so vital to the future of Israel. He also felt that Mapai had lost its erstwhile vision. Thus he was determined to turn the institutions of the new state—the government, and especially Zahal—into carriers of the lost vision which he sought to restore within new political procedures and institutions.

"The primary function of the ZHL has been to safeguard the state," Ben Gurion wrote. "However, this is not its sole function. The army must also serve as *an educational and pioneering centre* for Israeli youth—for both those born here and newcomers. It is the duty of the army to educate a pioneer generation, healthy in body and spirit, courageous and loyal, which will unite the broken tribes and diasporas to prepare itself to fulfil the historical tasks of the State of Israel through self-realization."

In 1949 these statements sounded more like prophecy than statesmanship. Time has vindicated Ben Gurion's vision of the army as a citizens' academy, the inculcator of public spirit.

NOTES

1. Ben Gurion, Preface, *op. cit.*, p. 54. (Ben Gurion's italics.)

2. See Reinhard Bendix, *Max Weber: An Intellectual Portrait* (Garden City: Doubleday, 1960), p. 302. On charismatic authority, explanation, and controversy, see recent literature on newly emerging political systems and their problems which has given a widespread use to the sociological term charisma which its originator, Max Weber, never anticipated. It has created confusion about Weber's own vision of charisma as well as about the significance and proper use of this concept in modern social scientific studies—especially in the field of political development. Although charisma was first used as a sociological term, as the sociologist William H. Friedland has pointed out, of the three of Weber's types of authority (bureaucratic-

legal, traditional, and charismatic), "... the traditional and the charismatic ... have been almost totally ignored by sociologists in empirical research." William H. Friedland, "For a Sociological Concept of Charisma", *Social Forces*, 43 (October 1964), p. 18. "For example, the *Index to the American Sociological Review* contains no category for 'charisma'. A search of various indices and journals reveals, indeed, that charisma has been utilized more by political scientists than sociologists." *Ibid.*, p. 18, n. 3. Part III, Chapter IX, of *Wirtschaft und Gesellschaft*, deals with the sociology of charismatic relationships. Selections from this chapter have been translated by Hans H. Gerth and C. Wright Mills in *From Max Weber: Essays in Sociology* (New York: Oxford University Press, 1946), pp. 245–52, 262–64. Max Weber's *The Theory of Social and Economic Organization* has been translated by A. M. Henderson and Talcott Parsons (New York: Oxford University Press, 1947) and presents Weber's authority types in English. Charismatic authority, routinization of charisma, and the transformation of charisma are discussed on pp. 358–92. Charisma is discussed also in Ephraim Fischoff's translation of Weber's "Religions soziologie" in the *Wirtschaft* under the title, *The Sociology of Religion* (Boston: Beacon Press, 1963), pp. 155–57, 269–74. See also Max Weber, "The Three Types of Legitimate Rule", *Berkeley Publications in Society and Institutions*, 4 (1958), pp. 1–11. A bibliographical note on Weber's works in German and their English translations is found in Bendix, *Max Weber*, *op. cit.*, pp. 9–12. According to Bendix, a complete bibliography of Weber's writings is appended (pp. 755–60) to Marianne Weber's biography of her husband, *Max Weber* (Heidelberg: L. Scheider, 1960).

3. This new information relating only Ben Gurion's point of view is found in his serialized memoirs beginning in *Ma-Ariv* (April 30, 1968). See Ben Gurion, "From the Diary", *op. cit.*, pp. 25–26. The basic points introduced here have already been made by Ben Gurion in preface, *History of the War*.

4. Interviews during the summer of 1967 with most members of Dayan's former General Staff (1953–1958), have convinced me of Dayan's clear understanding of the line between military and civilian responsibilities.

5. See Gordon Craig, *The Politics of the Prussian Army, 1640–1945*, 1966, especially pp. 193–219 and Walter Goerlitz, *The German General Staff*, 1953, pp. 64–102.

6. See the excellent analysis on the French High Command in David Ralston, *The Army of the Republic*, 1967, pp. 138–251.

7. Between 1948 and 1967 Israel had seven chiefs of staff, and all but two were under 40 years old when appointed. Among senior officers, mobility was similar to that of the junior officers and the average ages proportionately low: 40 to 44 for brigadier-generals, 35 to 40 for colonels, and 30 to 35 for lieutenant-colonels.

8. Ben Gurion, Preface, *op. cit.*, p. 54.

9. For an interesting study of the role of the kibbutz born in Zahal, see Yehudah Amir, "Sons of Kibbutzim in Zahal", *Megamot* (Heb.), Vol. 15, No. 2–3 (August 1967), pp. 250–58.

10. Eisenstadt, "Israel", *op. cit.*, p. 427.

11. The processes by which the Yishuv's institutional and social structures were depoliticized should be of interest to scholars concerned with political development and modernization. Israel could serve as an excellent case study and model for analysing the elements and parameters of political and social mobilization. The Israelis refer to the processes of national

F

integration since 1948 as *Mamlachtiout*. *Mamlacha* means kingdom and the analogy is taken from the Biblical reign of the Judges when the twelve divided tribes were finally united in the first Jewish kingdom. *Mamlachtiout* means the process of ingathering the Jews, political and social mobilization by the government, bureaucratization, formalization, and the integration of the immigrants. The conceptual framework for the study of *mamlachtiout*, or political integration, was laid by Eisenstadt in *Israeli Society* (New York: Basic Books, 1968), and *Absorption of Immigrants*, *op. cit.*; also in his "Patterns of Leadership and Social Homogeneity in Israel", *International Social Science Bulletin*, Vol. 8 (Fall 1959), pp. 36–53. The concept of political integration is closely linked in sociological literature with the concepts of political and social mobilization and modernization. The process of making a nation or a people "whole" or "entire", is found in the literature associated with the transfer of "old social, economic and psychological commitments" to "new patterns of socialization and behavior" (Karl W. Deutsch, "Social Mobilization and Political Development", *The American Political Science Review*, Vol. LV, No. 3 (September 1961), p. 494). This on-going dynamic and dichotomous conceptualization dominates the social sciences today. See Durkheim (mechanic-organic solidarity)—in Toennies (Gemeinschaft-Gesselschaft) Parsons pattern variables (universalism–particularism, etc.). See also T. P. Nettl, *Political Mobilization: A Sociological Analysis of Methods and Concepts* (London: Faber and Faber, 1967); Amitai Etzioni, *The Active Society* (New York: Free Press, 1968), pp. 388–422.

CHAPTER VI

Zahal's Role Expansion*

ZAHAL's extra-military functions—those activities not directly related to warfare—are a critical aspect of civil–military relations in Israel. In developing states, breakdowns in modernization, an uneven development in social and political mobilization, or inadequate integration have often created situations where the army must assume the tasks of managing and directing economic, agricultural, and educational enterprises. In such situations the army usually intervenes because of the absence, impotence, or indifference of other élites.[1] In Israel, however, there was *no* such modernization breakdown. The task of modernizing and integrating fell upon civilian organizations and the army simply complemented their work.

In Israel there is a reasonable and well-established reciprocity between the civilian stratification, economic, and political systems and the social and stratification systems of the army. In other words, the *exchange* of goods, services, and skills between these two sectors and the revolution in modern military doctrines has closed the gap between these two sectors. This is so for the following reasons:

(*a*) The rate of technological change has accelerated and a wider diversity of skill is required to maintain the military establishment.

(*b*) The diversification and specialization of military technology have lengthened the time of formal training required for mastery of military technology, with the result that the temporary citizen army becomes less important and the completely professional army more vital.

---

* For a sociological and political analysis of Zahal's role expansion' Professor Moshe Lissak, of the Hebrew University, and I have undertaken another book in which we plan to study the interplay and exchange of civilian and military personnel and resources in Israel.

(c) The complexity of the machinery of warfare and the requirement for research, development, and technical maintenance tend to weaken the line of organization between the military and the non-military. The result is that the differentiation between the soldier and the civilian is seriously weakened.[2] In all these trends, the model of the professional soldier is being changed by "civilianizing" the military élite to a greater extent than the civilian élite is militarized.——

Zahal's participation in nation-building was dictated by Israel's special needs:

> The involvement of Zahal in functions which are not purely military is no function of any particular ideology. It is not the desire on the part of Zahal to be an innovator but a condition of Israeli reality. The circumstances surrounding Israel demand a *pioneer army*; an army not bound by routine military functions but an army fulfilling nation-building functions. The army in a state of ingathering the immigrants must participate in this effort.[3]

Ben Gurion assigned Zahal many of the functions which had formerly been performed exclusively by the pioneers. In taking on these tasks, the army assumed the pioneer image as well. Thus the *esprit de corps* of Zahal was nourished by the pioneer legacy of the past.

In the realm of education, the argument for assigning Zahal the mission of ingathering and integrating Israel's mass immigration—between 1948 and 1955—was that it could penetrate areas either neglected or impenetrable by civilian authorities and other national institutions. The postwar immigrants lacked the political dedication, intellectual commitments, and organizational genius, characteristic of those who came prior to independence and consequently required more intensive indoctrination and orientation.

During this same period, the Defence Ministry expanded military-related industries which had been pioneered by the Haganah before and during the War of Liberation. Shimon Peres (1953–1965) guided the Ministry into the areas of applied military science and technology. Under his administration, the Defence Ministry took over the armaments industry, expanded the aviation industry, established the electronics industry, and forged ahead on nuclear research and development. Zahal officers and veterans play a key role in the management of all such enterprises and a special relationship between the Ministry and Zahal has developed as a result of this exchange of services.

The Defence Ministry and Zahal also co-operate with the civilian sectors of Israeli society in training manpower to meet the increasingly exacting requirements of new science and technology. Here the Defence Ministry, Zahal, and the civilian sector have formed an exchange system whereby each sector prepares manpower for the other.[4]

Education

) Zahal's educational activities can be broken down into two main types. The first embraces information, indoctrination, and entertainment programmes aimed at strengthening the civic and national consciousness of the recruits. The second category encompasses efforts to raise the level of manpower prior to induction and to ready soldiers and officers for smooth integration into society upon completion of military service.)

In 1952, a military specialization programme was proposed to complement the humanities, science, and agriculture programmes already existing in the high schools. This effort was to be tied in with the formation of a military academy, connected with Israel's foremost high schools, the *Reali* Gymnasium in Haifa and the *Herzelia* Gymnasium in Tel-Aviv.

Supporters of the proposal, led by General Yadin—then Commander in Chief—argued that the function of Israeli high schools was not only to train future scientists but also officers; that the training of officers was a civic function in Israel; and that military education at this level would raise the standards of Zahal's officer corps.[5] The proposal's critics—mainly senior high school teachers and members of the left kibbutz movement—argued that such a system would foster the growth of an army élite, a special class of officers, which would be contrary to the ideals of Israel. The controversy was resolved by compromise: the proposal for a military specialization programme in high school was dropped but a military academy was established in conjunction with the *Reali* School so that future cadets might "mix" with "civilians".

The flood of immigrants coming into Israel from the East had a great impact of the social and educational structure of the post-1950 army. The level of educational attainment of its officers was of special concern to the army. To close the educational gap within officer groups and between officers and conscripts, Zahal provided special schools to teach Hebrew and related subjects to newcomers. Women have figured prominently in this effort as teachers.

The army also moved into areas which were largely neglected by civilian authorities. This includes education among the lower classes and in geographically remote territories. Special attention was given to the educationally deprived, the high-school drop-outs, and the late developers, by establishing a special army educational centre—Camp Marcus, on Mt. Carmel, which was built in 1948, and trained 4,830 soldiers between1948 and 1950.[6] The drive to eliminate illiteracy in the army began in 1955. Elementary education—compulsory in Israel—was adopted by the army and was provided to 6,500 soldiers in 1966.[7]

Nahal

A no less important function of the army is played by Zahal's special army unit, the *Nahal* (Fighting Youth Movement) whose erstwhile leaders were former members of Palmach. The men in Nahal carry on the tradition of farmer-soldiers, working in border kibbutzim while serving in the army. Some kibbutzim are Nahal creations (Nahal-Oz, Almagor, and others) and frequently the servicemen remain in the border collective settlements (usually on the most sensitive spots at the Syrian or Egyptian borders) they have helped establish after discharge from the service. The Nahal currently plays a key role in settling the Israeli occupied territories in the Golan Heights (Nahal Golan) and in Northern Sinai (Nahal Sinai), Beisan Valley (Nahal Regev). Nahal also conducts special courses for agricultural instructors who are to assume leadership positions in new immigrant settlements.[8]

The Nahal programme, like Palmach, is composed of volunteers recruited mainly from the collective and co-operative agricultural settlements and from the pioneer Socialist youth movements in the cities. In purpose, ideology, and structure, the Nahal is modelled after the Palmach.

Like the Palmach, the Nahal conceives itself as the élite of the pioneer groups. The Nahal, however, does not serve as the reservoir *par excellence* of Zahal's office cadre as was the case with Palmach. The chances that Nahal recruits will continue their careers as agricultural settlers are far greater than the possibility that they will become officers.[9]

Nahal does not play in Zahal the role that Palmach played in the Haganah. Nahal was created in the spirit of the old agricultural pioneer settlements (before 1948) which regarded the kibbutz as an instrument to conquer the land. While the kibbutz and the Palmach movement served as the chief political and social mobilizers in Israel, Nahal and its kibbutzim are only one aspect of Zahal's role expansion. On the other hand, as Zahal's chief export to African nations, Nahal enhances the influence of Zahal in foreign affairs and has become a major supplier of military aid.[10]

Defence Industries

The Defence Ministry ~~adopted the Haganah tradition of self-sufficiency in weapon-making,~~ relying as little as possible on foreign weapons suppliers. This policy necessitated the formation of a sizeable industrial and scientific research complex which has developed weapons and techniques of warfare unique to the Israelis.[11]

The munitions industry originally developed as a branch of Haganah. Under the Defence Ministry it ~~has grown~~ GREW from a small-scale arms manufacturing operation into a highly complex electronics industry. The Ministry is engaged in both the production and purchase of weapons. These two functions have strengthened the Ministry's leverage with respect to the development and supervision of aircraft and electronics corporations, which are estimated to employ more than 20,000 people.

The army developed special technical schools and courses, designed to create a technologically skilled cadre to fill industrial manpower needs. The army also set up a special office (in connection with the Defence Ministry) for career counselling and occupational placement of skilled servicemen and officers.

This is to facilitate the absorption of army veterans into civilian society.

In 1966 the Air Force Technical High School was opened. The Air Force had been training technicians and laboratory men since its formation in 1948, and the opening of its own school attracted Air Force volunteers and guaranteed them a career after their service was completed.

The Defence Ministry's "invasion" into areas of technological modernization and private industry, especially electronics, and its control over industrial-scientific corporations connected with military functions, has been justified by the argument that only the Ministry could do the job. When Israel gained independence, its industries were small, with little capital to invest, and poor administrative talent. The Ministry, on the other hand, was financially and administratively capable of maintaining munitions, aircraft, and electronic industries even at high cost and loss. Critics of the Ministry claim that it has an efficient administration and that, being subject to civil service regulations, it is uneconomical for the Ministry to control all its extended functions.

Since the 1967 war the Defence Ministry expanded its electronics, aircraft, and missile industries. This is also a considerable contribution to economic growth and industrial modernization and proliferation in Israel. The slow and poor response of the private and some of the public sector to the orders of the Ministry again indicates the extraordinary role of the Ministry's advocates on the contribution of the military–industrial complex to economic modernization in Israel and above all the creation of greater capabilities for weapon autarchy on the part of Israel.

Control over Science

In Israel, science has always been closely tied to security. As early as 1947, the Haganah organized the Hemed (scientific branch of Zahal) which enlisted Israel's best scientists. The scientific army was inherited by Zahal but has since been incorporated into the Ministry of Defence. In this manner the production of nuclear weapons has been separated from the military proper.

In the area of nuclear technology and the application of atomic and nuclear energy to both peaceful and military uses, the Defence Ministry is the supreme authority. Israel's nuclear reactors and missile factories are subject to the Ministry's control and supervision.[12] Shimon Peres' greatest achievement was the development of the nuclear reactor at Dimona which greatly enhanced both his and the Ministry's reputation.

Zahal willingly surrendered the munitions industries and nuclear research and development to its civilian counterpart because they detracted from the army's efficiency and mobility. The fewer bureaucratic structures, argue Zahal senior officers, the more flexible the army.

Military and Society

Changes in the structure of the army élite in Israel have produced a remarkable change in its ideology. No longer does it entertain the political expectations of the Palmach or the NMO. It acts as one élite among others—an élite whose organizational tasks have been recruited to nation-building, economic modernization, and national integration.

The military élites have been diffused among the industrial-technocrats and bureaucratic élites of Israel. A tacit but highly institutionalized pattern has been established between the army and society. For the benefit of a vigorous and mobile army, officer turnover in Zahal is rapid; the society then absorbs the much-needed retired young officers. (See Table 7.)

The high requirements for efficiency and merit in Zahal naturally make Zahal's veterans a most desirable element in civic society. Zahal's graduates are achievement-orientated, and are pragmatic, experienced managers. The highly nepotistic Histadrut enterprises; the politically appointed senior civil servants; the government-dominated "private" co-operatives; and the politically orientated kibbutzim, all compete for the politically "neutral" and administration-orientated Zahal officers. Thus a Zahal officer develops an *alternative* career while still serving in the army. (See Table 8.)

Senior officers may take a leave of absence with the army's encouragement to study economic-administrative skills. The majority concentrate on economics, business administration, or

TABLE 7

Length of Service of Senior Officers in Zahal

Comparison of age of retired senior officers at the formation of Zahal in 1948 and their discharge in April 1966 and the same ranks still in the army.

Age	Senior Officers in 1948 (%)	Senior Officers Retired April 1966 (%)
22–24	8·7	
25–29	32·2	
30–34	23·5	5·2
35–39	20·0	26·9
40–44	7·8	28·8
45–49	3·5	15·7
50–54	1·7	6·1
55–	—	5·2
Unknown	2·6	12·1
	100·0	100·0

TABLE 8

Occupations of Retired Zahal Senior Officers
(Colonel and above) 1966

Politics	4·4
Ministry for Defence	5·2
Ministry for Foreign Affairs	6·9
Other Governmental Ministries	21·7
Government Corporations	12·2
Municipal Government (mainly as administrators)	2·6
Higher Education Institutions (administration and faculty)	5·2
Private Corporations	22·4
Independents	12·2
Return to Kibbutz	5·2
Other	2·0
TOTAL	100·0

operations research, either in Israel or abroad (Britain, France, United States). Others prepare for a law or university career. (See Table 9.)

TABLE 9 *Senior Officers in High Civil Service Posts*

Government Ministers 1968	Directors General 1967	Senior Directors	Defence Ministry Dept. Heads (30)	Foreign Office (28)	Government Corporations	University and Academia
M.-G. M. Dayan, Former Chf/ Staff, Def. (P)	Col. E. Amihad (P), Agricul.	B.-G. M. Limon (H) Ministry, Eur. Purch.	B.-G.—2 Cols.—15 L.-C.—8 Maj.—5	M.-G. I. Rabin (P), Amb. to US	M.-G. C. Laskov, Dir., Port Authority	M.-G. Y. Yadin, Prof. of Archaelogy (H)
B.-G. Y. Allon, Labor (P)	Col. O. Messer (P), Labor (Ret.)	B.-G. M. Goren (H), Former Dir. Purch. Misn. Gr. Brit. (Ret.)		B.-G. A. Remez (B), Amb. to London	Col. S. Lahal, Is. Airlines Co.	Col. Y. Neeman, Prof. of Physics (H)
B.-G. M. Carmel, Trans. (P)	B.-G. Avidar (H), Labour (Ret.)	Col. M. Mardor (H) Arm. and Sci. Dev.		B.-G. Y. Avidar (H), Amb. to Argentina (Ret.)	M.-G. Makleff, Dead Sea Co.	B.-G. Y. Harkabi, Prof. of Mod. Middle East Studies
I. Galeeli, Info. (P)	Col. Y. Pundak (H) Dep. Dir. Labour (Ret.)	Col. M. Prat (B) Nuc. React Div. (Ret.)		Col. A. Ben-Natan, Amb. to Germany	M.-G. Tsur, Water Desalination	B.-G. E. Pelad, Mod. Middle Studies
	Col. A. Ben-Natan (H) Def.	Col. S. Yiphtah, Nuc. Resch., Nahal Shorek (H)			B.-G. S. Shamir, Phosphates	Col. Yiphtah, Prof. of Physics
	M.-G. Z. Tsur, Former Chf/ Staff, Spec. Asst. Min. Def.				Col. Shamir, Aircraft	B.-G. Shoken (B) Registrar Tel-Aviv University
	Col. Moshe Kashti (H) Def.				M.-G. Amit (H) Chairman Kur Histadrut's major industrial concern	

Key: (H)—Haganah; (P)—Palmach; (B)—British Army.

It is impossible for a student of the military and society in Israel not to observe the close interplay between the two. No simple cry of an industrial–military complex could dismiss the subject. Nor could the pioneer legacy explain all the motives behind Zahal's role expansion. The organizational, administrative, and human resources of Zahal have been successfully exploited by Israeli society for its own expansion, industrial growth, and modernization. It is equally true that Zahal successfully exploits its image as heir to the pioneer and its high prestige, both of which raise the status of its officers in the eyes of the public.

Role expansion represents the equilibrium achieved by Zahal between its strictly professional functions and the voluntaristic legacy of its pioneer forerunners. The transfer of the functions of a mission-orientated community to a military apparatus and its bureaucratic structures and the interplay of two opposing orientations—professional versus voluntaristic attitudes—shaped this army in a way which could not have been predicted by either orientation. Zahal's role since independence has been charted along these patterns, neither of which has gained ascendancy over, nor excluded, the other. A typology of officers in Zahal could be established according to these orientations but would, of course, be beyond the scope of this study.

NOTES

1. See Moshe Lissak, "Modernization and Role Expansion of the Military in Developing Countries: A Comparative Analysis", *Comparative Studies in Society and History*, Vol. IX, No. 3 (April 1967), pp. 233–55. I am grateful to Professor Lissak for ideas, advice, and help in developing the theme of this chapter.

2. See Morris Janowitz, *The Professional Soldier* (New York: Free Press, 1960), pp. 347–442; Janowitz and Roger Little, *Sociology and the Military Establishment* (New York: Russell Sage, rev. ed. 1965), pp. 9–26.

3. *Bamachane* (Zahal's weekly) (February 15, 1951), p. 16.

4. This has also been true of the American army since World War II, where most electronics, radio, and television technicians receive their training.

5. On the controversy and the views of General Yadin and others, see *Bamachane* (February 28, 1952), pp. 3, 16. Also consult *Ha-Aretz* during the same period.

6. "Camp Marcus", *Bamachane* (July 20, 1950), pp. 7–8.

7. *Bamachane* (October 29, 1967), p. 10.

8. *Bamachane* (May 5, 1955). In 1966 the Nahal organized its first

industrial cadre to work in the newly built Negev city, Arad. On the relations between the army and the Youth Movement, see Etzioni, "Israeli Army", *op. cit.*, pp. 6–7.

9. On Nahal's training programme and participants, see Irving Heymount, "The Israeli Nahal Program", *The Middle East Journal*, Vol. 21, No. 3 (Summer 1967), pp. 319–24.

10. A list of Nahal programmes in Asian, African, and Latin American countries is found in Heymount, *ibid.*, p. 314. See also I. Oron (ed.), *Middle East Record 1960* (London: Weidenfeld and Nicolson, 1962), pp. 302–303, 306–15; and *Middle East Record 1961* (Tel-Aviv: Israel Oriental Society, 1967), pp. 333–44.

11. On defence industries and their relation to Israel's economy, see Sir Leon Bagrit, "The Modernization of Israel", *Ha-Boker* (April 4, 1965); Zeev Shiff, "Controversies in the Defence System", *Ha-Aretz* (August 12, December 14, December 21, 1966); Philip Offer, "Between the Army and the Civilians", *Ha-Aretz* (November 20, 1963); General Chaim Hertzog, "Industry and Security", *Ha-Aretz* (March 25, 1966); Y. Elitzur, "Invaders to the Civilian Industries", *Ma-Ariv* (January 4, 1963).

12. The Atomic Energy Commission and its directors are employees of the Defence Ministry.

CHAPTER VII

The Institutionalization of Civil–Military Relations in Israel

THE BEN GURION LEGACY AND ITS CHALLENGERS
(1953–1963)

The Era of Consolidation: The Lavon Affair

THE struggle for political power in Israel in the decade and a half between 1953 and 1968 took place over Israel's defence and foreign policies. The most bitter struggle was over the control of the defence ministry and over Zahal. Once the established Israeli labour movement and its power structures, Mapai, Histadrut, and Kibbutz, were well institutionalized, the arena for wielding political influence became the defence ministry and the control over Zahal.

The struggle for power (especially after Ben Gurion's short retirement, 1953–1955) within the ministry demonstrated the nature of civil–military relations established in Israel. The struggle was over (a) the scope and functions of the defence minister *vis-à-vis* Zahal's high command but particularly the chief of staff; (b) the organizational structure of Zahal and of defence's military–industrial complex; and (c) the type of war conducted with the Arabs (thus the type of weapons system used by Zahal). This culminated in the formation of a legacy firmly institutionalized by Ben Gurion: the minister of defence as chief of war and the chief of staff as its chief tactician, the high command as his advisers; the subordination of Zahal and its high command to the civilian minister; the division of labour between Zahal and the ministry's industrial-nuclear system again subordinate to the defence minister; the search for peace with Arabs independent from a policy of maximum modernization of Zahal, its structural organization and *esprit de corps*, in preparation for the next campaign.

The 1949 armistice failed to produce a peace treaty with the Arab nations as some Israeli policy-makers had hoped and optimism gradually gave way to recognition that the armistice had become, *de facto*, a permanent condition of Arab–Israeli relations. The unwillingness of the Arabs to co-operate with Israel on its terms and their dedication to pursuing the conflict in even more radical ways caused the Israelis to develop a policy in view of Arab encirclement.* This policy emanated from the defence establishments in order to secure Israel from "another 1948", and was eventually institutionalized as Zahal's chief strategic and political doctrine.

Intense political struggles over the destiny of Zahal and the future course of international and Arab policies have always been linked to Israel's security. In the years 1948–1955, the main strategists of Israel's defence policy were Ben Gurion and Zahal's high command. Zahal was assigned operational responsibility for many crucial defence policies and, therefore, in its successful pursuit of these operational goals, Zahal's strategy could determine to a large extent the course of Israel's foreign relations. Zahal became identified with national security; and national security became identified with Arab encirclement.

The Lavon affair and crisis in the Defence Ministry grew out of Ben Gurion's special treatment of Zahal and the Defence Ministry in applying a strategy against Arab encirclement. During his tenure, the division of power between the military and the bureaucratic and political structures of the Defence Ministry remained largely undefined, although the pre-eminence of Zahal over the Ministry was tacitly understood. When Lavon succeeded Ben Gurion as Defence Minister and attempted to control strategic policy-making and also dominate tactical policy, wresting this power from Zahal's high command to himself, he upset the unofficial balance Ben Gurion had

* I am using the term Arab encirclement in the same sense that the Soviets use the term—as an instrument of foreign policy. To the Soviets (especially during Lenin–Stalin reign) the West represented a capitalist encirclement while to the West during that period the Soviets represented the menace of Bolshevik world domination. Thus to the Israelis the physical surrounding of Israel by belligerent Arab states represents an Arab encirclement while to the Arabs the establishment and existence of Israel and Zionism in the midst of the Arab world is an imperialist conspiracy.

established in the Ministry on security matters, and thus Lavon stirred up a nest of hornets in the process.

The Lavon affair is the most conspicuous representative act of constraint upon civil–military relations in Israel. It demonstrates how a political rivalry between the defence minister and Zahal's high command was resolved within the higher political order, the civilian arena—the ruling party Mapai, the cabinet, the general public—and not within the military establishment itself. The affair, which rocked Israeli politics, shook up Mapai and aroused the most vigorous private and public criticism of Ben Gurion and Zahal's defence strategy, was in the end resolved by civilian authorities.

The Ben Gurion–Dayan Arab encirclement strategy and the debate over defence and foreign policy were contingent on Mapai's and labour parties' internal rivalries, since the Palmach's dissolution, and on Ben Gurion's manipulations. The dynamics of nationalization and formalization of Zahal posed a challenge to many pioneer-founders of the state, who sought to infuse the ideology of pioneer Zionism into the institutions and practices of the state and in the army. From their institutional strongholds—Mapai, Histadrut, and the kibbutz movement—they struggled for influence and position against Ben Gurion's nationalization efforts by protesting against "bureaucratism", "the desertion of pioneer values", and "the betrayal of socialism". They viewed the formalization of Zahal as a victory for Ben Gurion's nationalist design—*Mamlachtiout.*

The Lavon affair represents the friction in the relationships between civilian and military authorities in Israel before they were finally institutionalized and a definite pattern evolved. The controversy revolved around the scope and function of the minister of defence, the chief of staff and the high command. The conflict over the issues of war and peace, and the clash over interpretations of Israel's Arab policy held by Israeli political and military élites coincided with an institutional crisis in the Ministry. Thus, key terms and policies intermingled with each other—Arab encirclement, retaliation, preventive war on the one hand; patient diplomacy, penetrating the Arab wall of hatred, and conciliation on the other. The former gained priority in the defence establishment led by Ben Gurion and Dayan while the latter were supported by Moshe Sharett, the

Foreign Minister who led a group of Mapai–Histadrut and left kibbutz–Mapam leaders. These fundamental issues on war and peace were *closely* connected with the future structure of Zahal, its equipping and purchasing procedures. All were directly related to the scope of decision making and the division of labour between the minister and his chief of staff.

In the controversy over defence policy, Ben Gurion's opposition failed to trap him into a potentially damaging ideological campaign. In large part, this was also due to Arab stubbornness, the widening of the Arab–Israeli conflict, and changes in Middle Eastern politics which occurred in the early 1950s.

The following developments gave unexpected strength to Ben Gurion's position and the stand of the "hard-liners" in Israel: Nasser's assumption of full power in Egypt, after two controversial years, in 1954; the failures of the Egyptian–Israeli *rapprochement* in 1953–1954; the acceptance of Western aid by Iraq and the conclusion of the Baghdad Pact in 1954; the increased flow of Western arms into Iraq; the Dulles doctrine of treating the Arab states and Israel "equally" which tipped the balance in favour of Arab "progressives" led by Nasser; the military support offered to Egypt in 1955 by the Soviet Union and Czechoslovakia; Soviet support of the Arabs in the UN Security Council; the barring of Israeli shipping from the Suez Canal and Egyptian seizure of the Israeli ship *Bat Galim*; the Cairo anti-Zionist trials and the beginnings of conflict with Syria over the diversion and use of the water of the Jordan. These events were enough to suggest the possibility that the Arab states, led by Egypt, would mount a new military assault against Israel. The moderates argued that such an attack was not probable, but the situation nevertheless gave credence to the argument that the army should be used to ensure peace through the judicious use of force—which meant retaliation and increased readiness for war.

The years 1953–1955 were therefore critical for Israel's defence and security systems. These were years of great personal and institutional changes in ~~Zahal~~ and in the Ministry where crucial political decisions were taken, determining Israel's defence posture for a decade.

The radical change in the balance of power in the Middle East; the pro-Arab policies pursued by the Soviet Union which had earlier sponsored the establishment of Israel in the United Nations, especially the deterioration of relations between Israel and the Soviet Union; and the rise of Nasser's junta to power in Egypt, intensified and sharpened the conflict between the hard-liners and the moderates in Israel. Each group interpreted internal and external events in a way calculated to gain political and public support for its policies.

The debate extended from the top echelons of the Ministry and Zahal's high command to the political parties, the parliament, and the press. The division over the future of defence and foreign affairs became bitter and at times seemed irreconcilable; the duel was fought over the Israeli policy of retaliation.

The Chiefs of Ministry and Zahal saw Arab encirclement and intransigence as dangerous to Israel. They advocated and pursued a strategy of directly confronting the Arabs along the borders in the hope that this show of determination would eventually bring the Arabs to the peace table. This group was cohesive (supported and surrounded by Ben Gurion) and was in actual control of the means to carry out their policies.

Moshe Sharett, the Foreign Minister, was the most influential and effective spokesman for the Israeli moderates, who unlike the hard-liners, were not cohesive and were ideologically divided. He was sharply critical of the Ben Gurion–Dayan policy of retaliation and border raids (mainly because of several failures early in 1950–1952) although he was not opposed to the strengthening of Zahal and its military aggrandizement. Sharett advocated adopting an attitude of conciliation toward the Arabs thereby hoping to strengthen the position of moderate leaders in the Arab world. He held this view despite Egypt's rearmament policy, believing that Israel had not exhausted all means for bringing about an Arab–Israeli *rapprochement*. What he feared most was that Israel would force the great powers to take action. He was also concerned about the possible damage that retaliation could do to Israel's relatively good standing in the United Nations and in Western public opinion.

The leftists especially those in the Mapam party went further than Sharett—they hoped and believed that Arab–Israeli reconciliation could take place if and when the repressive Arab régimes were replaced with progressive and Socialist type governments. The rise of Nasser gave them such a hope. The moderates wanted to curtail border raids so as to make Israel's foreign policy more flexible.

Ben Gurion, challenged by the moderates in the cabinet and in the party, especially over border raids, prepared to resign rather than compromise his position, hoping that once the policy pursued by the moderates was exhausted, his view would prevail. Ben Gurion did return to power after a 15-month absence but for reasons other than even he anticipated.

In November 1953 Ben Gurion resigned, and on December 7 he left for his newly adopted Negev kibbutz Sdeh-Boker. In his place, he appointed a brilliant Mapai-Histadrut theoretician and orator, a man little connected before with defence matters, but now a dedicated Ben-Gurionite, Pinhas Lavon. One day before his resignation, Ben Gurion also appointed Maj.-General Dayan to become Zahal's Commander-in-Chief. At the time Lavon was named Defence Minister, Shimon Peres was appointed Director General of the Ministry. Thus Lavon was buttressed by two old "defence hands", especially Dayan, the most politically conscious of Zahal's commanders since 1949 (after the mass resignation of Palmach officers).

Foreign Minister Sharett was appointed Prime Minister. Ben Gurion hoped that his trio could successfully isolate Sharett and other opposition in the cabinet and successfully carry the doctrine of Arab encirclement into operation, short of jeopardizing the chances for his return as Defence Minister. Thus a new era was launched. The three, competent in their own realms, were also strong personalities and ambitious politicians, each jockeying for position.

Initially, both Dayan and Peres catered to Lavon, but they soon discovered that an alliance between them, a division of labour between their offices (probably inspired by Ben Gurion in Sdeh-Boker), and adherence to Ben Gurion's policy, could isolate Lavon whose daily interference in their offices they resented. During Ben Gurion's tenure, they had run their offices practically without interference.

In the past, Ben Gurion had viewed with sympathy the actions of his "boys" and had given the commander in chief practically a free hand in determining Zahal's tactics and actions. He had let the high command handle such questions as the rectification of borders; maintaining pressure on the Arab armies; and drawing the attention of the world (especially the West's) to Israel's border and security problems. Dayan left Zahal's economic, supply, and financial matters to the Ministry, and the co-ordination which resulted between the two enhanced the role of the Ministry.

In 1954 it appeared that Zahal and the Defence Ministry had finally reached a stage of effective co-operation. Dayan and Peres had established close relationships mainly based on a friendship of convenience directed to first restrict Lavon and later to topple him. Although Peres bowed to Dayan's primacy, it was during this same period that he built up the Ministry's prestige by turning it into a large-scale military supply organization. Dayan enhanced Zahal's reputation and effectiveness in carrying out the border raids policy. He also initiated a large-scale reorganization of Zahal and the formation of special units, paratroop and commando, to carry border raids successfully and lift Zahal's morale after several border raid failures. Peres reorganized and expanded the Ministry to meet the need for rapid rearmament and Zahal's expansion and modernization in order to prepare Israel for a "second round" with the Arabs.[3]

Pinhas Lavon was not a behind-the-scenes man. He was a strong and ambitious politician in his early 50s, a former leader of the Mapai youth movement and Gordonia, and prominent in the settlement movement and in Histadrut. His appointment was blessed by Ben Gurion, who saw in Lavon a true champion of his defence policies and conception of Zahal's role. Lavon indeed started his tenure as a militant, but he faced great difficulties from the outset.

In his desire to enhance the Ben Gurion activist policy and to outdo his former master, Lavon not only intensified the strategy of retaliation but added a new dimension to activism. The chief technician of the strategy of retaliation, Dayan, resented Lavon's meddling in what he considered to be purely army business. Dayan insisted on separation of the civil and military realms. Lavon persisted in pursuing Ben Gurion's vision of fusing military policy under the minister of defence. Lavon further antagonized the loyalists by failing to "consult" the Ben Gurion "experts" on tactical matters and by interfering in military details especially his detailed study and personal involvement in border raids actions. Thus he only encouraged the internal intrigues—not necessarily sponsored by him—among civilian in the Ministry and officers in Zahal.

Lavon also meddled with military policy by activating various of the Ministry's sabotage files. This was in connection with unsuccessful raids. Although most of these files had been prepared by the Aman's and Mosad's intelligence divisions under Ben Gurion, now military and intelligence officers were not only disregarded but, on behalf of a "new policy", supplanted. In this fashion Lavon hoped to gain control over the Ministry, Zahal, and Ben Gurion's loyalists in the Ministry and among Zahal's intelligence divisions.

The fifteen months (December 1953 to February 1955) of Ben Gurion's retirement were thus characterized by a growing estrangement between Lavon, Peres, Dayan, and Zahal's high command. The deep division in the cabinet concerning the course of defence and foreign policies, which had culminated in Ben Gurion's resignation, were now further widened. The trio Lavon–Dayan–Peres accelerated Ben Gurion's policies while Sharett and the cabinet opposed the policy of retaliation and border raids.

Lavon made little effort to share the functions of defence with the cabinet. His aim was to act as Ben Gurion did—as the chief and only authority in security matters. Here Lavon remained isolated both from the cabinet and from Zahal. The senior command led by General Dayan carried on with a retaliation and Lavon could not count on the support of Sharett or of the cabinet since he was a well-known member of a "hawkish" clique. Pressing for direct and daily co-ordination between Zahal and the Ministry, so that he could dominate Zahal's high command, Lavon further antagonized the commander-in-chief, who threatened resignation.

Lavon's failure to ally himself with the army and his rejection by the Ministry specialists and bureaucrats (tacitly organized by Peres) forced him into more radical directions than he would have charted otherwise. Rather than resign, he became embroiled in security misfortunes, not of his own doing, which in the end cost him his career.

Sometime in 1954, a series of Israeli espionage and sabotage operations in Arab countries (Egypt and Syria) collapsed, thus bringing to an end one of Israel's greatest spy rings in Egypt. This has since been called the Fiasco (*Ha-Esek ha-Bish*).* A secret *ad hoc* committee was appointed by the Prime Minister Moshe Sharett to investigate the espionage débâcle. This committee—the Olshan–Dori Committee—was established with the active support of Lavon.

The already tense relations between Lavon and Dayan–Peres reached a new phase over the Fiasco. Lavon's independent investigations in preparation for the *ad hoc* committee hearings were resisted by the intelligence division of Zahal whose efforts, under the leadership of Colonel Benjamin Jibly,† Chief of Army Intelligence, were directed toward implicating Lavon with responsibility for the Fiasco. Some intelligence officers even forged documents and testified against him before the committee. At the same time, Shimon Peres, in his testimony before the committee, concentrated on Lavon's incompetence as Defence Minister. In this way, the hearings were turned from a challenge to the army intelligence division's competence and responsibility for the Fiasco into Lavon's trial.

Lavon was astonished to learn that his understanding with Sharett—on the nature of the Olshan–Dori Committee's investigation—had been broken and that without his consent the scope of the investigation had been broadened to include a probing into the relationships between the Ministry and Zahal. In vindictive testimonies, both Peres and Dayan strayed from the Fiasco to comment on Lavon's incompetence as Defence Minister. But Sharett did not budge and in the end, in the interest of national unity and security and preserving the good name of Zahal's officer corps and protecting Zahal's morale, the 1954 committee reached no conclusions and condemned no

* For security reasons we are unable to discuss in detail the security operations which led to several fiascos, but in particular a mishap in Egypt. We are aware that several journalists from the *New York Times* to *Le Monde* "told" some of the story. In view of the information at our disposal most of the above journalistic stories border with the fictional and resemble suspense stories rather than the much simpler series of failures which brought about the fiasco. On the other hand, the charge of the monstrosity that Israeli intelligence committed in Egypt is more complicated than the fictional stories offered by "reliable" journalists.

† Jibly was involved in another fiasco in the past—the Tobiansky Affair of 1950. As deputy chief of intelligence he was instrumental in the execution of Tobiansky as a spy after a hurried court martial.

one, not even the cabal of intelligence officers who actually plotted the dismissal of Lavon, although it did note that some documents were forged and that one of the intelligence officers lied to the committee.

The decision of the Olshan–Dori Committee left Lavon more isolated than ever. This decision not only failed to weigh in his favour but implicated him with the Fiasco, and there is no evidence that he had any responsibility except for his own concern for several unsuccessful raids. Lavon demanded that Sharett should dismiss Peres and the intelligence officers who plotted against him, but Sharett refused for the same reason that the committee reached a tie decision. Lavon demanded large-scale institutional reforms in the Ministry, thereby dissolving Ben Gurion's legacy. He demanded: the strengthening of the authority and control of the minister by buttressing the civilian sections of defence; firm rules on the scope of office and relationships between the Ministry and Zahal; the creation of a national security council composed of both civilian and military members which would act as the highest security authority in times of peace; the formation of a higher control system over the army and the Ministry and several other reforms.[4] Sharett refused to accept these recommendations and Lavon finally resigned.

On February 22, 1955, Ben Gurion returned to his post as Defence Minister, while Sharett remained in his post as Prime Minister until Ben Gurion took over this office on November 4, 1955. In 1954 the Israeli public was unaware of the Fiasco, which was guarded as top secret until 1960. We shall return later to the consequences of the 1954 Fiasco which came to a head with the Lavon affair of 1960–1961.

It is obvious that Lavon was insensitive to the patterns of behaviour and the institutional and personal interactions and procedures of the Ministry. He was brusque, impatient, and above all succeeded in less than a year in alienating friend and foe alike. A group of rivals plotted against him, without the backing of the Prime Minister, who considered Lavon the leader of the Ben Gurion clique when he was actually their major target. Either Lavon did not understand or perhaps did not have enough patience for the special relationships and procedures of his office. He had underestimated the quality of Ben

Gurion's power and legacy and that of Dayan and Peres. Nor did he take advantage of the convenient Dayan–Peres political alliance the purpose of which was to bring about his downfall. Why hadn't the Olshan–Dori Committee investigated the Fiasco more thoroughly? Didn't this create a situation favourable to an alliance between plotters and rivals—each group, for different reasons, dedicated to behead the minister?

In concert with the Prime Minister and the cabinet, the committee was more concerned with Israel's security problems and maintaining Zahal's high morale than with structural reforms in the Ministry which Lavon, under different circumstances, would not have concerned himself about either, caught by the Fiasco and the rivalry within the intelligence division. The committee refused to meddle in the machinations of the intelligence division, fearing that it might demoralize an important arm of Zahal. It is presumed that the committee hoped that the tie decision and the inconclusive recommendations would be enough to urge the army to purge the plotters. This is what happened when Ben Gurion came back to office. Colonel Jibly was removed and so were a few others in the intelligence division. Thus, national interest prevailed.

Prime Minister Sharett, not a powerful man, could hardly have been expected to render support to Lavon, his rival. If anyone had to be the victim it was Lavon. The committee and the cabinet fully appreciated the extraordinary qualities of Dayan and Peres, who were tacitly (and even openly) supported by Ben Gurion in Sdeh-Boker. In fact, he was consulted several times by Sharett and Mapai chieftains on the Fiasco, on the committee's recommendations, and on Lavon's capability of running the office. Effective support for Lavon from Mapai and the cabinet simply was not forthcoming. He was now viewed by his colleagues as a failure.[5] In fact, some had attempted to persuade Ben Gurion before his retirement in 1953 not to appoint Lavon as his successor, as Defence Minister.

It might also be asked how the morality of Zahal could be upheld in view of the dishonesty of some of its intelligence officers. Here, however, politics prevailed over military morale considerations.

Lavon's recommendations for a total reform of the defence establishment of which several recommendations were pertinent and should have merited high consideration, especially those relating the fixed jurisdictions and duties of several key posts, were put aside and dismissed by Ben Gurion when he returned to office. These were also ignored because reform of the Ministry would have implied vindication of Lavon, among others.

Lavon's proposal for the formation of a mixed military–civilian national security authority to oversee the Ministry was doomed. The lessons of Haganah and Palmach dictated it futility and how unrealistic it was in the case of Israel. Such a body obviously would have become political and the traditional political party system established in Histadrut, in the kibbutzim, in Mapai, in the cabinet, and in all of Israel's political and economic structures would have turned Zahal back to the pre-independence era, when military structures were instruments for political influence. Under that system, a chief of staff would not be selected by merit but on a political basis and the chances for the emergence of politically inclined officers and compromise candidates (whose military and professional standards would not be requisite) would be enhanced. This situation duplicated on the lower levels of the army would have dissolved the great achievement of Zahal's unification, professionalization, and depoliticization. Thus Lavon's recommendations, if accepted, would have brought professional and moral disaster to Zahal.[6]

Another important reason for rejecting the recommendation for a national security council was that it would have made the army's swift and lightning action—Zahal's military doctrine—ineffective. It is for this purpose that Dayan relieved Zahal of most of its administrative, logistical, and armament functions, so that the army could achieve a swift and highly mobile force.

February 1955–September 1960

When Ben Gurion assumed office after the Lavon crisis, he was confronted by (1) a radical change in the balance of power in the Middle East in favour of the Arabs; (2) a Soviet–Czech–Egyptian arms agreement; (3) a Nasser-dominated Egypt which had become seriously involved in the Palestine conflict; (4) the pro-Arab policy adopted by the Soviets strengthened the hands of the militants in the Arab world. Nasser's breakthrough and the optimism of the new wave of Arab nationalism supported by two major powers enhanced the Arab militants' view that they eventually could bring about Palestine's liberation.[7] Thus his tasks were:

1. To modernize and aggrandize Zahal which was now being equipped with the help of Israel's new ally, France.[8]

2. Because the *rapprochement* with revolutionary Egypt had failed,[9] to apply organized retaliation to Gaza, the Palestinian territory occupied by Egypt since the Arab–Israeli war. This explains the February 28, 1955, Gaza raid only six days after Ben Gurion took office. It was in retaliation for the seizure of the ship, *Bat Galim*, in the Suez and the execution of the Jewish spy ring in Egypt. Here the Ben Gurionists won the upper hand. The Gaza raid did not create a new pattern of events, it was part of a trend which had begun months before.[10]

3. To expand the Ministry's scientific and armament industries and develop a nuclear capability in Israel in the hope of eventually deterring the growing Arab military forces.

4. To foster close co-operation with France—Israel's only major supplier of weapons and a centre for Israeli scientific–nuclear training.

5. In view of the Fiasco, to initiate reforms in Zahal by curtailing responsibility for retaliation on the part of the middle and junior officers and instituting strict supervision by senior officers of all retaliation operations; cleansing the intelligence division and appoint an intellectual and an Arabist, Colonel (later Brig.-General) Yehoshafat Harkabi, to head army intelligence.

The years 1955 and 1956 were frantic in preparation for a forthcoming clash with the Egyptians. The die was cast for the Sinai war after the Egyptian–Czech arms deal and Dulles's Northern Tier Middle Eastern defence scheme. As Ben Gurion saw it, there was no way out. Not that he advocated a Second Round but he bowed to the dictates of the realities of a growing Arab encirclement.

The Soviet entry into the Middle Eastern arena with its heavy arm supplies to Egypt and other Arab countries convinced Ben Gurion more than ever that an Arab–Israeli showdown was forthcoming and that the militants in Egypt had gained the upper hand. What he wanted therefore was to *surprise* the Arabs so that he and not Nasser would dictate the time and place for the next Arab–Israeli confrontation. In these efforts he found the services of Dayan and Peres invaluable. He could not have chosen two more capable and loyal disciples.

After the muddles and fiascos of 1954, the sporadic and organized mutually recriminating retaliation and border incidents, *Bat Galim* and the execution of the spy ring in Egypt, and, above all, the uncertainties of Israel's national security, there was a psychological victory at Sinai even if Nasser reaped the fruits politically. The morale of the nation and the morality of the armed forces, its dedication, professionalism, and good conduct confirmed Ben Gurion's belief in Zahal's good name despite the Fiasco and the immoral behaviour of *isolated* intelligence officers. The nation, unaware of the Fiasco, rejoiced in Zahal's victory. The prestige of General Dayan and Zahal and of the Defence Ministry and its Director General, Shimon Peres, were enhanced. The lessons of Sinai dictated the aggrandizement of the Ministry's supply and scientific and industrial enterprises.

Since Sinai, the defence establishment has become the chief client of Israel's technological and scientific achievements. It has invaded the private market as well as large-scale modernization enterprises. Next to Histadrut and the civil service, it has become Israel's chief employer. Here it threatened the civilian industrialization enterprises of Israel. Criticism came from various directions triggered by the threat of an industrial–military complex; the invasion of military men into the managerial class; the destruction of civilian infant industries; and the danger of the Defence Ministry becoming an autarchy, harnessing industrial developments and the free market, etc.

The Ministry argued that autarky in industry and science for defence purposes was a must in Israel and that it did not threaten established industries but pioneered new industrial and scientific enterprises such as the aviation and electronics industries. The Ministry's aggrandizers prevailed, under the dynamic and mobilizing leadership of Peres, supported by Ben Gurion. Dayan's doctrine that Zahal should not be burdened with the problems of supply and production also enhanced the aggrandizement of the defence "empire".[11]

The Lavon Affair and the Decline of Ben Gurion
(October 1960–1963)

In the summer of 1960, the 1954 Fiasco became the Affair. Late that summer, Lavon approached Ben Gurion on the 1954 matter, claiming that he had gathered "fresh" information that would prove his innocence, and requesting that Ben Gurion publicly exonerate him. Ben Gurion ordered his adjutant to investigate Lavon's new information and the veracity of the intelligence officers' testimony. In September, Ben Gurion told Lavon that he was unwilling to reopen "the wounds of 1954", but offered to investigate the question of who gave the order for the "disastrous action" that year. He thus ordered the Commander-in-Chief, General Chaim Laskov, to investigate the charge against the intelligence colonels. Ben Gurion appointed this Zahal committee without Lavon's knowledge or consent. On September 25, after the public announcement of the appointment of Laskov's army committee, Lavon met Ben Gurion again; he protested that in view of his "new findings" there was no need for another investigation, and requested that the committee be dissolved and an announcement of his exoneration be made.

It had now become evident that there were more issues than exoneration involved. Both Ben Gurion and Lavon opposed resolving the matter within the party. Lavon continued to demand from Ben Gurion a public announcement of his innocence. Ben Gurion, for his part, claimed that he was neither judge nor prosecutor, stating, "I have not implicated Lavon and it is not my duty to exonerate him and if somebody else implicated him, his rehabilitation is not within my authority". Now the sabotage affair, the workings of the inner sanctum of the Defence Ministry, and Ben Gurion's system of political control, had all become topics of public discussion; the politics of defence, but not its doctrine or Zahal's strategy, had become a national controversy.

On December 25, a cabinet committee formed to investigate the Lavon affair submitted a report which offered the following conclusions: (1) Lavon had not "given the order"—the sabotage action had been executed without his knowledge or authorization. (2) The committee could not determine what the exact working relations were in the Ministry of Defence in 1954. (3) The committee accepted the attorney general's report that certain documents presented before the 1954 committee were false.

The government accepted the cabinet report; no minister opposed it, although some abstained (Ben Gurion did not participate in the meeting, General Dayan, Minister of Agriculture, abstained from voting on the matter). Ben Gurion announced that he would not accept the cabinet committee's opinion as binding on him, and would accept only the decision of a judicial committee.

In response to growing public concern an Intellectuals' Committee was formed, composed of Hebrew University professors in Jerusalem, led by Professor Jacob Talmon (author of *The Rise of Totalitarian Democracy*) and Nathan Rotenschtreich, a philosopher, Mapai intellectual, and Lavon's colleague from the youth movement days. This committee protested public character assassination and the "personality cult" prevailing in Israel, which it said posed "a growing and disturbing threat to the Israeli democracy". Professor Talmon wrote a two-page article in *Ha-Aretz* (March 1961) which analysed the affair, and concluded with a call for "greater public moral responsibility".

Ben Gurion threatened to resign, thus forcing Mapai into new national elections only two years after the bitter campaign in 1959, in which it had lost more than 5% of its previous majority. A serious party split could have brought an end to the unchallenged supremacy the party had held since 1935. As a state party, Mapai concentrated on unifying itself and preserving its coalition government and its control in the Histadrut.

For the first time since 1935, a major political realignment seemed possible. As they became better defined, nation-building processes, previously delegated to the House of Labour, were gradually being taken over by the bureaucracy and the departments of the new state. The struggle for power between the institutional leaders and the founders of the state, against their most natural successors, the modern corporate bureaucracy and the army élite, gained momentum during the affair.

In this struggle against the whole state apparatus and its power élites, especially Mapai's, Lavon was doomed. It had become clear to Mapai leaders that Lavon could cause the party to suffer heavy electoral losses and possibly even to lose its control of the government should Ben Gurion resign. This being the situation, Mapai's Executive Committee in the cabinet (*Sarienu*) decided to act against Lavon to pacify Ben Gurion and protect the party. On February 5, Mapai's Central Committee passed a resolution which removed Lavon from his position as Secretary General of the Histadrut. The vote was 159 for, and 96 against, with 5 abstentions; and Mapai's Executive Committee, acting on the advice of the Central Committee, mustered a 28-to-11 majority to support Lavon's ousting. Defeated, Lavon resigned.

Although Ben Gurion remained at the helm of party and government, his prestige had suffered. In a famous "5,000 words" speech, he called Lavon's challenge "an open war against defence, a profane attack on the holy Army of Israel". The speech ended with an admission of what had been the crucial issue, Mapai's maintenance of power:

> The unity and purity of our party and the future of the state of Israel are interdependent. And I hope that you [members of Mapai] remember to keep the two always in your minds.

The Lavon affair might have precipitated far-reaching and revolutionary changes in Israeli society, politics, and the military. Among the possibilities were a major political realignment; reorganization of the defence establishment; more efficient parliamentary supervision of the Ministry and Zahal; public and press criticism of the defence establishment; and removal of the defence establishment from the foreign policy arena.

Despite the shock which the 1960–1961 affair produced in Israel, no great changes took place. Mapai, with Ben Gurion at its head, lost a small percentage of votes and a few seats in parliament,[12] but electorally and institutionally it weathered the storm. No substantial institutional reforms were made in the defence establishment; cabinet and parliamentary control over the defence establishment was not increased or tightened; nor were the efforts of the "imperialistic" aggrandizers in the Ministry curtailed in any way. On the contrary, the defence establishment's industrial and scientific empire continued to expand its roles and functions. Although no major or revolutionary changes occurred in the highly institutionalized and centralized governmental and economic enterprises in Israel, or in the basic conservatism of the Israeli voter, the cumulative effects of the affair between 1961 and 1965 resulted in the attrition of Ben Gurion's power and influence. It also set into motion a growing public and political debate on the role of the defence establishment and concern for the protection of Israel's democratic values, and ideals.

The affair was not the only reason for the awakening of intellectual and public criticism. At the same time, there was increasing recognition of and public dismay over the meagre political fruits secured from the military victory in Sinai. The affair sharply delineated the cumulative changes which Israeli society had undergone since independence. It demonstrated the problems emerging out of the radical change from a voluntaristic, cohesive, and highly mobilized society with effective and competing autonomous political and economic institutions to a national bureaucratic, compulsory, and highly centralistic political and economic system—all controlled by the state, its enterprises, and bureaucracy dominated by labour. The only independent and autonomous politico-economic structures, which were themselves centralistic, monopolistic, and paternalistic, were the Histadrut and kibbutzim enterprises. The widening gap between the political, economic, and bureaucratic élites in Israeli society[13] became a political issue.

The affair created a wedge within Israel's ruling party, Mapai, and in the Histadrut. The champions of each group clothed personal and institutional rivalries and the protection of vested interests with national and ideological symbols. Thus the defenders of Lavon in Mapai, Histadrut, and the kibbutzim, called for the dissolution of the authoritarian and etatist (the term most frequently used) military–industrial complex; for the regeneration of pioneer and co-operative values supposedly arrested by the military establishment; closing the gap between the two Israels (that of the old Yishuv and the new, which included immigrants from African and Asian countries); and the return to the "sources" of pioneer and "democratic" values. Lavon and his followers organized themselves into a faction of Mapai called From the Foundation (*Min Ha-Yesod*) in order to bring political pressure from within the HOL and Mapai on the government and on society.[14] The most important political effort of this group was to challenge the activist–Ben Gurionite leadership and his allies in the party, government, Histadrut, and in the bureaucracy. The Lavonites demanded large-scale, basic, and revolutionary changes in the defence establishment, which were mainly based on Lavon's old outline proposed to Sharett and Ben Gurion in 1955. This challenge, the affair, and pressure from the public and press created turmoil within the party; old rivalries were renewed, new ones were created.

In defence of the military establishment, the Ben Gurionites claimed that the Ministry and Zahal demonstrated cohesion and efficiency during the short, but successful, Sinai Campaign; that the retaliation policy had been vindicated by that campaign where Zahal demonstrated the skills learned in the border raids; that the aggrandizement of the Ministry's scientific and nuclear enterprises bolstered Israel's deterrent to Arab aggression; that Zahal's role expansion demonstrated its function as a nation-builder and inculcator of the civic spirit and democratic ideals; that Zahal's moral stature and heroic role serves as the ideal that the pioneer symbolized in the pre-state era;[15] that the defence establishment had pioneered and carried the major burden of economic and scientific modernization in Israel; that in the new highly rational nuclear age, the Ministry's industrial complex and Zahal, rather than Histadrut and Mapai, should serve as a model.

The conflict of age versus youth also became an issue. The Ben Gurionites said they represented the latter, although Lavon's faction claimed great influence among university students and Israel's young intellectuals, as well as a considerable number of the other young élites.[16] Closer to the truth is the fact that Israel's youth and intelligentsia were divided between the two and that the Ben Gurionites had no monopoly on youth.

The elections of 1965 dispelled once and for all the myth that Ben Gurion spoke for the youth; his splinter party received only a small percentage of the total vote (7·9%) which is far below the size of that age group in Israel.[17]

The Lavon affair obsessed Ben Gurion. He called for a one-man crusade against the "detractors of the sacred Zahal".[18]

Unable to mobilize and rally the party, the Histadrut leadership or the cabinet behind his Lavon crusade, Ben Gurion resigned on June 16, 1963.

Eshkol, who had actually negotiated the formation of the 1961 cabinet, succeeded Ben Gurion as Premier and Defence Minister. As was the case with Lavon, Eshkol was appointed by Ben Gurion, who considered him his *alter ego*, at least throughout the Lavon controversy. In the end, the thaw in the Israeli political establishment began with the affair.

NOTES

1. Major-General Moshe Dayan, "Israel's Border and Security Problems", *Foreign Affairs*, XXXIII, No. 2 (January 1955), pp. 250–63.

2. An analysis of this period is found in Shimon Peres, *Ha-Shavlav Haba* (*The Next Phase*) (Heb.) (Tel-Aviv: Am Hasephar, 1965), especially pp. 9–15.

3. Yoseph Evron, *Beyom Sagrir* (*The Cold Years*), Tel-Aviv, Otpaz, 1968, is based on Peres's diaries.

4. For sources see the Tel-Aviv daily, *Ha-Aretz* (June–September 1955, and June 1960–April 1961); the Tel-Aviv fortnightly *Ma-Ariv*; and *Davar*, the Histadrut–Mapai daily for the same periods. Ben Gurion's statement in *Ha-Aretz* (January 13, 1961), p. 2; Lavon's Histadrut farewell speech, *Ha-Aretz* and *Davar* (February . 5, 1961). Author secured information through personal interview with Lavon and his colleagues and with members of the Defence Ministry who prefer to remain anonymous; information also secured from the author's personal friends among senior Zahal reserve officers. See three controversial volumes on the affair: Ben Gurion's apologetic *Devarim Kehavayatam* (*Things. as They Are*) (Heb.) (Tel-Aviv: Am-Hasepher, 1965); Y. Arieli's *Ha-Kenunya* (*The Intrigue*) (Heb.) (Tel-Aviv: Kadima, 1965), in Lavon's defence; and Hagi Eshed's "The Affair", *Ha-Aretz* (February 19, 1965), in Ben Gurion's defence. For a general description of the 1954 affair, see E. Hasin and D. Horwitz, *The Affair* (Heb.) (Tel-Aviv: Am-Hasepher, 1961). This is the best analysis of the affair and is inclined to accept Lavon's view.

5. Interviews with Lavon; also see Hasin and Horwitz, *The Affair*, p. 79.

6. This is not always true in other countries where civil–military relations and national peril are less urgent than in Israel.

7. In the opinion of UNTSO head, General Burns, an impartial observer, although not very sympathetic to Israel, the Arab argument that time is on their side strengthens the hands of Nasser and Arab militants; E. L. M. Burns, *Between Arab and Israel* (New York: Ivan O. Bolensky, 1963), pp. 30–31.

8. On Israeli–French relations and the policy of arms purchase, see Michael Bar-Zohar, *Gesher 'al Ha-yam ha-tichon* (*A Bridge Over the Mediterranean Sea*) (Heb.) (Tel-Aviv: Am-Hasepher, 1963).

9. Earl Berger, *The Covenant and the Sword: Arab–Israeli Relations 1948–56* (London: Routledge & Kegan Paul, 1965), pp. 173–75. Even an Arab-inclined interpretation of the Arab–Israel retaliation policy admits the

H

institutionalization of permanent retaliation by Egypt since 1955. See Fred J. Khouri, "The Policy of Retaliation in Arab–Israeli Relations", *The Middle East Journal*, Vol. 20 (Autumn 1966), p. 440.

10. Berger, *The Covenant*, p. 175. Earl Berger summarizes clearly Israel's optimism regarding the Egyptian revolution. Thus the retaliation policy was formerly concentrated on Jordan and Syria and not applied to Egypt. The Israeli retaliation policy was applied to Egypt when this optimism faded in view of Nasser's commitments to the Palestine conflict, see pp. 168–69, 165–203.

11. The debate for and against the Ministry's aggrandizers is still carried in the press. In defence, see Hertzog, "Industry", *op. cit.*; Offer, "Between the Army", *op. cit.* For criticism see Bagrit, "The Modernization", *op. cit.*; Zeev Shiff, "The Danger of Operational Entanglement in Zahal", *Ha-Aretz* (August 14, 1966); Elitzur, "Invaders", *op. cit.*

12. In the Fifth Knesset Elections (1959) Mapai lost 3·5% of the vote (34·7%) since the Fourth Knesset Elections in 1955 (38·2%). They lost five seats (47 to 42)—the lowest since the 1951 elections.

13. See S. N. Eisenstadt, "Israel", in Harold M. Rose (ed.), *The Institutions of Advanced Societies* (Minneapolis: University of Minnesota Press, 1958); and Moshe Lissak, "Patterns of Change in Ideology and Class Structure in Israel", *The Jewish Journal of Sociology*, Vol. VII, No. 1 (June 1965), pp. 46–62.

14. Lavon's faction also founded a monthly *Min Ha-Yesod*. The first issue of the above (1962) covers most of the ideological and political claims of this faction.

15. See Ben Gurion, *Things as They Are*; Shimon Peres, *The Next Phase*, several articles by Ben Gurion, Dayan, and Peres in *Ha-Aretz* and *Ma-Ariv* between 1961 and 1967, Rafi party's journal *New Outlook* (*Mabat Ha-dash*) published since 1965. The interesting phenomenon in Israel after the Six Days' War of June 1967 demonstrates that the anti-etatists and Lavonites were not vindicated nor was the course of Sharett and Lavon espoused by the youth or the intellectuals. Although no empirical and statistical study has been made I venture to offer the following hypothesis: that Israeli intellectuals—poets, writers, journalists, scientists, and *some* university professors—advocate a militant policy concerning Israel's occupied territories, some arguing for their immediate annexation; while the military establishment and the high command advocate the establishment of *secure* and easily defended frontiers in preference to all-out annexation. See *Ma-Ariv* interview with Generals Rabin and Yadin (February 16, 1968). In my field research trip to Israel in the autumn of 1967 I interviewed several members of Zahal's high command and middle echelon officers and have found their position as that of Generals Dayan (interview with *Bama-chane*, March 10, 1967), Rabin, and Yadin. The university community, faculty, and students are differently divided. This is beyond the topic in this study; but on the whole I hypothesize that the intelligentsia (government bureaucrats and journalists) and the "belle lettrists" have demonstrated greater militancy than Zahal's high command, senior army veterans, and the university communities in Jerusalem and Tel-Aviv.

16. Professor Fein's excellent analysis of Israel's politics did fall prey to the ideological slogan of youth versus age put forth by Rafi claiming that Mapai was dominated by old men. See Leonard Fein, *Israel* (Boston: Little, Brown, 1967), pp. 157–58. The fact was that in the 1960–1963 Ben Gurion cabinet three were five Mapai members below 50—Allon, Dayan, Sapir,

Eban, and Peres. The 1965 cabinet had three men in key positions—Eban, the Foreign Office; Allon, Labour; Zadok, Trade; and Sapir, Finance, who were just a little over 50.

17. Ben Gurion's speech before Mapai, *op. cit.*

18. Ben Gurion's statement in *Ha-Aretz* (January 13, 1961), p. 2.

CHAPTER VIII

Eshkol's Term of Office as Defence Minister (June 1963–June 1967)

RELATIONS between the Mapai–Histadrut party leadership and the élites of the defence establishment deteriorated. In March 1964, Ben Gurion wrote a controversial article in *Ha-Aretz* attacking both Generals Yadin and Allon for failing to conquer "the complete Palestine" in the 1948 war. Had Dayan been Chief of Staff, Ben Gurion claimed, the "map of Israel would have been different".[1] Ben Gurion was rebuffed by both generals who argued that as Commander-in-Chief, he could have elevated Dayan to that position. Invoking his concept of the defence minister as the head of war, they charged that he was responsible for the curtailed "map of Israel" (and its unsatisfactory borders)* and not his subordinate generals.

The controversy snowballed when Eshkol asked Lavon to return to Mapai's chief councils and Executive Committee on May 2. Nine days later Dayan resigned as Minister of Agriculture, citing lack of "identification" with Eshkol's cabinet.[2] Ben Gurion demanded the reopening of the Lavon affair and Eshkol resigned to demonstrate his opposition. In December 1964 the cabinet, led by Eshkol, rejected the "reopening of the Lavon affairs",[3] but the party, Histadrut, and the HOL were split over the issue. The 1965 elections clouded the issues and sharpened the divisions with Mapai and the HOL. At the Tenth Party Conference in Tel-Aviv on February 8–10, 1965, the Mapai–Histadrut old guard, Meir, Aran, Sapir, and Sharett, persuasively attacked Ben Gurion. Ben Gurion persisted in demanding the reopening of the affair, while Eshkol and the old guard favoured its closure. The bureaucracy in the Defence Department were also torn between admiration and

* This is, of course, before the Six Days' War in June.

respect for Ben Gurion and his position and recognition of the party's political strength and electoral success. At the party conference, the Ben Gurionists organized a faction, the New Power (*Ha-Koach he-Hadash*), led by Dayan and Peres and Mapai's Haifa's boss Abba Hushi.

In the struggle for control over the party Executive Committee and the party conference, Ben Gurion's forces mustered 40% of the party behind them, while the Eshkol forces could count on 60%. On the question of removing the Lavon affair from the party's agenda, 1,226 (58·1%) of delegates approved with 848 (41·9%) against. On the issue of forming the Alignment, a parliamentary and electoral alliance with the United Labour Party (which defended Lavon and whose leader was Dayan's rival—General Allon), 1,306 (63%) of the delegates approved, while 770 (37%) opposed. The kibbutz movement, the co-operatives, and the party in Tel-Aviv supported Eshkol. Only the delegates from Haifa and the new Negev settlements (most of whom represented employers or were employed by the Ministry of Defence and the government) supported Ben Gurion's faction.[4]

Upon conclusion of the party conference, the battle between Ben Gurion and Eshkol continued to be waged in Mapai, in Histadrut's central councils, within the councils of Histadrut's economic enterprises, and in the Ministry of Defence and its enterprises—only Zahal was spared the rift. Zahal was prohibited from participating in party politics; however, it is to be assumed that Zahal's high command and its officer corps (except officers affiliated to United and National Kibbutz Movements) favoured the Ben Gurion–Dayan faction.

The clash was intensified in the high councils of government and within the Defence Ministry enterprises following the party conference in February 1965, due to violations of the civil service law which prohibits the participation of civil servants in politics (the Director General of Governmental Offices and the senior staff are on the whole political appointees).

In January 1965, Lavon was ousted from the party and Dayan and Peres attempted to mobilize all their influence, power, and political leverage to nominate Ben Gurion as the party's candidate for premier. In an article in *Ha-Aretz*, Dayan called for activism in defence in view of the Jordan River conflict between Israel, Jordan, and Syria.[5] Ben Gurion labelled Eshkol "incompetent" and a "lag" in the defence establishment. Peres proclaimed that "Peace with the Arab countries could be achieved only by strengthening of Zahal" and that the Generation of Sinai (after 1956) was not adequately represented in the party.[6] Ben Gurion's challenge failed on June 4, 1965. By a vote of 179 to 103, the party Central Executive Committee named Eshkol over Ben Gurion as its candidate for premier in the 1965 elections.[7]

Ben Gurion refused to let the Lavon issue die. He inspired the Hagi Eshed article in *Ha-Aretz*, and his own speeches, articles, and pamphlets called once more for the reopening of the affair.[8] On May 20, 1965, Shimon Peres, the Deputy Minister of Defence, resigned from the cabinet. In August 1965, the party membership committee, at the behest of the Executive Committee, recommended that Ben Gurion be ousted from the party. On November 4, Dayan, under pressure from Ben Gurion, resigned from the party, and on November 15, 1965, Ben Gurion, the founder and leader of Mapai since 1929, added his resignation. The Ben Gurion–Dayan–Peres group founded a new electoral party, *Rafi*.[9] (*Rafi* refers to the Alliance of Israel's Workers.) This signalled the end of Ben Gurions' reign over Israel.

Rafi claimed to represent Israel's new and young generation; calling itself the forerunner of modernization in Israel; advocating the rationalization of Israel's paternalistic bureaucracy; taking credit for pioneering in defence and Israel's nuclear development; in short, calling itself Israel's best representative for the future. When the vote was in, Rafi had won less than 8%, barely ten members to parliament.[10] Thus from a most powerful position within the Mapai–Histadrut coalition and domination over the defence establishment and its senior civil service, the Ben Gurion faction declined into a small party, losing its influence in the HOL and in the country—completely at the mercy of Ben Gurion.[11]

Eshkol's decisive victory[12] was not a victory for the moderates in the defence establishment, nor for the pre-independence Socialist–co-operative ideologists. Lavon and his allies had already been ousted. Eshkol did receive the backing of Israel's modernization élites in Histadrut, the defence establishment, retired army officers, key civil servants, industrial managers, and the intelligentsia. This was demonstrated by the composition of the pro-Eshkol volunteer organization ATA (the abbreviation for Civilian Support of Eshkol) which wielded influence in Israel's economic–defence–industrial establishment. Although Israeli political positions before 1948 were basically ideological, the struggle for power and influence over the state, key HOL structures, and control of Mapai was based more on *personal* and *institutional* rivalries than on ideologies. This tended to mar the real issues at conflict.[13] It was not a rivalry of youth versus age or ideologues versus pragmatists (*Bitzuistim*); etatism versus democracy; or civilians versus the military—Mapai and Rafi actually represented all of these polarities, but Rafi clothed itself in a pragmatic ideology. Rafi condemned Mapai as a traditional, "corrupt" and nepotist political organization. While calling for "party democracy", this faction was simultaneously instituting a highly centralized system in the defence establishment! Peres, its head, condemned Histadrut's monopolistic tendencies and behaviour, while at the same time supervising the aggrandizement of the Ministry's enterprises. He challenged Histadrut's expansionism, condemning Histadrut and Mapai for nepotism, filial piety, and particularistic practices, while employees of the Defence Ministry were recruited in the same way. Peres called for a politically free and efficient civil service, overlooking the fact that the Ministry was full of politically appointed, inefficient, and "corrupt" civil servants. Rafi claimed that Histadrut's managerial class lacked modern vision, and an industrial–scientific education, while some of the administrators in the Ministry of Defence and the bulk of the top-level defence industries personnel were not even high school graduates, including Peres, the director general.

The clashes in the political arena were actually surface demonstrations of similar struggles going on within the fabric of Israeli society as the processes of integration conflicted with the rapid modernization and growth of scientific and nuclear enterprises. The trio of Ben Gurion–Dayan–Peres became the scapegoat for grievances against the defence establishment.

In response to public pressure, Peres' successor as Deputy Minister under Eshkol, the economist, Dr. Zevi Dienstein, attempted to *streamline* the Defence Ministry by divesting itself of several departments, such as recruitment, armament, and supply, and transferring them to the army. Led by Chief-of-Staff, Maj.-General Yitzhak Rabin, the army remained steadfastly loyal to Dayan's view that Zahal should be unburdened by such support functions. Zahal's doctrine of swift warfare militated against Dienstein's plan which was only partially adopted.[14]

A devotee of American-style cost efficiency, Dienstein hoped to strip the Ministry of all functions save one, financial control over defence operations. This would have given the Ministry power to dominate the army. Zahal refused to go along, however, under the pretext that these reforms would transform its carefully selected and highly trained officer corps into "merchants" and "clerks"—occupations which Zahal's high command regarded as beneath their dignity or outside their responsibility as warriors.

Eshkol's reign was characterized by Zahal's most prosperous growth. David Ben Gurion and Moshe Dayan were experts on military affairs and needs and while, on the whole, they satisfied the military, in several instances, they *overruled* the high command's requests for greater budgets. Levi Eshkol was no military expert and he depended on General Rabin for advice on Israel's military needs. Eshkol, as Finance Minister under Ben Gurion to 1963, intervened between the army and Ben Gurion by cutting the defence establishment budget, especially in the field of nuclear development. Eshkol, the Defence Minister, with full control over finances as well (through his control over Sapir, the Finance Minister), failed to pull his weight against the aggrandizement of Zahal and complied with General Rabin's requests for expensive new weapons.[15] With the demise of old security hands, Ben Gurion, Dayan, and Peres, Rabin's influence over security matters was greatly enhanced.

The departure of Ben Gurion created a vacuum. Eshkol lacked the personality to inspire the charismatic and personalistic relationships with his subordinates which Ben Gurion had used so effectively during his long tenure as Defence Minister. These qualities, however, were not in such demand as they had been during Zahal's formative years. At this point, the defence establishment was well institutionalized and functionally proliferating; it had become a large and effective machine with a momentum of its own, following the patterns established over the course of two decades. In fact, one could well argue that, in the course of time, the patterns established by Ben Gurion were so well incorporated in the routine that even when he himself strained these patterns, as he did through the years 1960–1965, when he meddled with the affair, he failed to challenge the legacy he had established.

The aggrandizement of the defence establishment in a nation mobilized for what amounts to a permanent war, as Israel is, only makes the need for civilian control over the military more imperative. Eshkol is hardly admired by Zahal's high command nor, for that matter, by numerous other bureaucratic and intellectual élites, but relations between him and Zahal were cordial and correct and never in the history of civil–military relations in Israel has the principle of civilian domination of the military been better established. The crisis in government before the 1967 June War fully demonstrated this; the relationship weathered serious challenges from both without and within. But Eshkol's type of domination was bitterly challenged during Israel's most formidable crisis between April and June 1967.

Since 1961, Israeli–Syrian non-relations further deteriorated. With the rise of the Ba'th Party to power in 1963, and radical Ba'thists and the military takeover of the party in 1966, the Syrian border was the scene of the most bitter friction between Israel and the Arabs. This Syrian group turned into the most belligerent Arab extremists since 1948. This development, coupled with Israel's determination to divert the waters of the Jordan River and border clashes with Jordan, escalated mutual recrimination culminating in a severe Israeli air attack on military installations near Damascus on April 17, 1967.

Ben Gurion and other Rafi militants demanded Eshkol's resignation. Ben Gurion declared in public and in the press that Eshkol was not fit to govern, charging a credibility gap in defence matters (*Mehdal Bithoni*). The government's effort to streamline Peres's empire was represented by critics as a political calamity causing a severe lag in military preparedness, especially in the nuclear field, which of course could only be remedied with the return of Ben Gurion and Rafi to office.

While Zahal enjoyed its most prosperous era under Eshkol, as the 1967 victory clearly demonstrated, and while Rabin is said to have influenced Eshkol's decision to retaliate against Syria,[16] Ben Gurion, Isar Arel, the former head of *Mosad* (General Intelligence), Shimon Peres, and lesser Rafi stalwarts vehemently attacked Eshkol for "betrayal" of Israel's security posture.

This was the prelude to the 1967 war. The attrition due to the Lavon Affair culminated in a real realignment of political forces in Israel. This was demonstrative *only* after June 1967. However, the legacy of Ben Gurion in the defence ministry survived. In fact, the rise of Dayan and the behaviour of Zahal during the months of crisis, May–June 1967, demonstrated the persistence of the type of civil–military relations in Israel established by David Ben Gurion.

NOTES

1. *Ha-Aretz* (March 10, 1964), p. 2.
2. W. Granger Blair, "Dayan Quits Post in Israel's Cabinet", *The New York Times* (May 11, 1964).
3. *The New York Times* (December 28, 1964).
4. The statistics are taken from *Ha-Aretz* (February 17–18, 1965).
5. *Ha-Aretz* (March 26, 1965).
6. Press conference reported in *Ha-Aretz* (May 2, 1965).
7. *The New York Times* (June 5, 1965).
8. See footnote 3, Chapter VII, on Eshed and Ben Gurion polemics.
9. Many hoped that it would threaten Mapai into capitulating in order to maintain its position as Israel's leading party.
10. This party, in essence Mapai's New Power faction, founded in the February Party Conference, which then represented 40% of the party's Central Committee, received only 7·9% of the popular vote.
11. An unpublished study of the Hebrew University demonstrates that Rafi was successful among the 18–25 age group. But the so-called Histadrut–Mapai youth and heirs (*Dor Ha-Hemshech*) are the 38–53 age group. An impressive 60% of this age group, the study demonstrates, voted for Mapai.
12. The alliance of Mapai and United Labour won a high 36·7% of the vote (45 seats), the highest for Mapai since the formation of the state.
13. On the ideological transformation in Israel see Moshe Lissak, "Patterns of Change", *op. cit.*, pp. 46–62; and Eisenstadt, "Israel", *op. cit.*, pp. 384–443.
14. On Dienstein's Grand Plan, see Shiff, "The Danger", *op. cit.*
15. My interpretation of the relationships between the Defence Minister and Zahal is based on personal interviews with the high command, active and retired, and the Ministry's senior civil servants. It is obvious that, for security reasons, the type of budget required and the nature of its aggrandizement cannot be revealed here. It should be mentioned, also, that the figures published by London's Institute for Strategic Studies concerning the Israeli army were not confirmed by the June 1967 war; some numbers were,

at best, wild guesses. The general trend of Eshkol–Zahal relationships can be found in the Israeli press of this period, especially the Friday issues of *Ha-Aretz* and *Ma-Ariv*, and *Yediot Aharonot*.

16. See last footnote.

CHAPTER IX

The Role of General Moshe Dayan
(June 2, 1967–   )—Some Speculations

THE heightening of tensions between Israel and the Arab world over the Syrian call for the immediate liberation of Palestine, the Soviet penetration in Egypt and especially in Syria, American preoccupation with Vietnam, Nasser's growing restlessness and suspicion of American estrangement from Egypt, and the British withdrawal from Southern Arabia all contributed to the Middle East tinder-box which erupted in the brief Six Days' War of June 5 through 9, 1967. The dispersal of the UN Emergency Force, Egyptian mobilization in Sinai, and the closing of the Gulf of Aqaba for Israeli shipping made the conflict inevitable. It ended in disaster for the Arabs with Israel occupying parts of Syrian, Jordanian, and Egyptian territories, from the heights of Mt. Hermon to the Suez Canal, and in control of the west bank of the Jordan and the integration and unification of all Jerusalem.[1]

Our interest in the war is limited to the question of how Dayan became the Defence Minister and why Eshkol, stubborn at first, had no choice but to relinquish Israel's most important portfolio—the Defence Ministry. Dayan assumed the position of Defence Minister on June 2, under most extraordinary circumstances.[2] An impatient and anxious Israel, inundated by a barrage of threatening Arab propaganda and sensing American indecision and reluctance to uphold their commitment to maintain Israeli security, needed a psychological morale booster. Wanting reassurance, the public forced the return of the "hero of Sinai", Moshe Dayan. It is inconceivable that he would have been called to this office under any but these dire circumstances so long as the septuagenarian trio of Eshkol–Meir–Aran reigned over Mapai.

Israel's crisis of confidence was brought on by a combination of the following developments and several misconceptions: (a) the reluctance of the Eshkol trio to meet Nasser's challenge head on, hoping instead for a diplomatic respite as evidenced by Eban's disappointing missions to France, and the United States;[3] (b) the failure of the Mapai leadership to quell pressure from its "Continuing Generation" élites (ages 38–53), influential in the upper and middle echelons of the party, government, and the Histadrut, for Dayan's return; (c) the resistance of the party hierarchy to creating a broad national coalition; (d) the organization, by Rafi Secretary General Shimon Peres, of opposition to the government which effectively broke the cabinet's collective responsibility—this included a Mapai minister and other prominent party members, *Gahal*, the chief opposition party (the Alignment of right—General Zionists and Herut), and *Mafdal* (National Religious Party), a member of the Alignment coalition government; (e) the effective mobilization of public opinion, organized by *ad-hoc* committees for national unity and by the press led by *Ha-Aretz*, a politically moderate but nationalist daily; (f) Eshkol's lack of resolution and loss of public confidence and support; the adroitness of Moshe Dayan in making himself "available" only in the event of popular demand. In the end, these factors converged to force Mapai to create a national unity cabinet, representing all parties but one of Israel's two small Communist parties.

Eshkol and the Mapai party hierarchy had at first been determined not to relinquish their control over the defence establishment and were adamant in their refusal to widen the coalition government, a move which would weaken their position. Eshkol even excluded the possibility of offering the Defence Ministry to General Allon, a pillar of the Alignment coalition who, as a former commander of the Palmach, and a veteran expert in security matters, was the most qualified candidate for the office. As the crisis escalated, Eshkol's intransigence and monopoly over defence came under mounting criticism from public and press who demanded he widen the cabinet to achieve national unity.

Dayan's name was first mentioned by the press. Menahem Begin, former commander of the NMO and the leader of *Gahal*, went personally to the home of his lifetime opponent Ben

Gurion, to offer him the premiership. Ben Gurion, however, refused to serve in a cabinet which included Eshkol and proposed Dayan for the office of Defence Minister instead, to which Begin agreed. Taking his cue, Shimon Peres suggested a Rafi–Gahal–Mafdal coalition as an alternative to the Alignment cabinet.

Learning that Dayan, their most bitter rival had been proposed for the defence office, the Eshkol trio bowed to public and party pressures and offered Dayan what he actually demanded later, the command of the Southern Front (claiming that he knew best how to defeat the Egyptians). In this way they hoped to neutralize Dayan and avoid appointing him Defence Minister. General Rabin, Zahal's Chief of Staff, was approached and accepted Dayan as his subordinate. But the public, the press, and the organized opposition (led by Rafi) demanded that Dayan be awarded the Defence Ministry.

Several weeks before the war, Dayan had requested permission to review Israel's military plans and began this by touring the troop facilities in the Negev. Many of the soldiers and the reservists enthusiastically cheered his return. This was related to the rest of the country through the press, and public pressure to appoint Dayan as "Israel's Saviour" eventually forced Eshkol's hand. Thus the hesitation, lack of resolution, stubborness, and inability of the Mapai hierarchy to perceive public opinion[4] lost them the Defence Ministry and returned to power their most formidable rival.

Three days later, the newly appointed Defence Minister, General Dayan, ordered Zahal to strike. Undoubtedly, war plans had been prepared well in advanced of Dayan's order and whatever changes he might have made were minor. By symbolizing national unity and resolve to win, however, the "hero of Sinai" reaped all the fruits of victory. Dayan received the credit for what had actually been a permanent and continuous effort of the Israeli people, government, and military strategists, to which the Eshkol administration and Rabin's leadership had made a most significant contribution. The world press—*Time*, *Newsweek*, *L'Express*, and *Der Spiegel*—anointed Dayan as the hero of that brilliant campaign and his dashing "pirate-like" appearance was propagated by right and left journalists alike. Lacouture, of *Le Monde*, called him a legionnaire.[5]

The real Dayan, the cautious and supreme political tactician and thinker, has been obscured in the flurry of publicity. His "non-colonization" policy toward the west bank is highly acclaimed in Israel and abroad. He demonstrated caution in not opening a third front against Syria until the fourth day of the successful Six Days' War. In a series of articles appearing in *Ha-Aretz* and *Ma-Ariv* in recent years, he has written on foreign policy, defence matters, and Middle Eastern and international politics. Since the June War, Dayan has clearly formulated Israel's defence and foreign policies: in negotiations with Arabs the emphasis should be on security rather than territorial acquisition; coexistence with the west bank; channels of communications with the Arab world through the Palestinians; maximization of Arab local government (in view of occupation which at best is not the type of rule preferred by the west bank Arabs); turning the Jordan River into a centre of communication and commerce between Arabs in occupied territories and the Arab countries so that the citizens of the Western Jordan could become the go-between for Israel and the Arabs in the future; eventual political solution with the Palestinians.[6]

As a political tactician, he has proved superior to Eshkol whose reputation is based solely on his aptitude for politics and making compromises. Not unlike Eshkol when he became Finance Minister, Dayan, as Minister of Agriculture, recruited university-trained experts to run the Ministry of Agriculture. He has also done this in his drive to reorganize the Defence Ministry.

While Dayan's image was enhanced as the undefeated hero and national saviour, the image of Eshkol as an indecisive man continues to plague him and weaken his grip over the national unity government; Eshkol never quite regained the public's or his party's confidence. The present situation is to *some* extent reminiscent of 1954. The deep gulf between the Prime Minister and his Defence Minister has weakened the collective responsibility and the actions of both. But the differences between 1967 and 1954 are also great: Eshkol, the ageing (73), hesitant, inarticulate, grey and hard-working compromiser, is no *real* competition for the dashing, younger (53) hero of two wars, Israel's new charismatic leader, Dayan. The new Ma'i party— uniting Mapai–United Labour and Rafi—which was established in January 1968, obviously strengthens the hand of Ben Gurion's heir-apparent and disciple, Dayan. It also has restored Eshkol's image and restored the power of Allon, now deputy prime minister. In another way 1967 is different from 1954. Eshkol depends on Dayan to buttress the pressures coming from cabinet members, especially Allon and Alignment allies; the relationships between the Minister of Defence and the Chief-of-Staff, Maj.-General Chaim Bar-Lev are close and cordial and Zahal is a more efficient and cohesive military machine than it was in 1954. And above all, there is no constitutional dispute on the clearly established and separate roles of the minister and the chief of staff.

As Defence Minister, Dayan perpetuates the patterns of civil–military relationships established by Ben Gurion over two decades ago. Like Ben Gurion, Dayan is at once an effective and domineering civilian administrator and a superior military expert. Under him, there has been a fusion and intimacy between civilian and military élites in the defence establishment with acceptance of the supremacy of the former. He has wielded great influence over Zahal both in his capacity as commander-in-chief and as a hero who inspires and who is emulated.

Dayan, in whose image officers of Zahal were moulded during his tenure as Chief of Staff (1953–1957), found his friends and junior subordinates had moved up to the middle and upper echelons of Zahal's officer corps. The graduates of Sinai are now on Zahal's senior staff and several of these officers distinguished themselves in the 1967 war. The policy of rapid officer turnover has produced a new crop of officers with battle experience. General Sharon is, at present, the only officer in the high command with no pre-Zahal training and a disciple of Dayan. Within the next two years, however, it is expected that at least five colonels, most of whom are the heroic type[7] who distinguished themselves in 1956 in Sinai and during the Six Days' War and all of them Zahal graduates and Dayan's disciples, will be promoted to brigadier-general and some will become members of the high command by 1970.[8] Maj.-General Chaim Bar-Lev, the new Chief of Staff (January 1968) and his senior colleagues Brig.-Generals David Elazar (Dado), Yeshayhu Gavish, and Rehavam Zeevi are former Palmach veterans but over the next five years the Palmach reservoir will have been exhausted. Thus, in the next decade, Zahal's high command will become dominated by its own graduates, the veterans of the wars of 1956 and 1967.[9]

Since 1967, most Zahal senior officers, especially the divisional commanders, belong to the Zahal graduates group and are Dayan devotees as is the case with several corps commanders. For this reason it is anticipated that Dayan's tenure (short of a crisis in the national unity cabinet or a radical change in its composition after the 1969 elections) will launch one of the most intimate eras in Israeli civil–military relationships. Contrary to the views of some unregenerated professional anti-militarists in Israel or abroad, we venture to predict that Dayan will prove the value of establishing a dialogue between the chief architects of Israel's security and foreign relations and Zahal's high command. As Ben Gurion's long regin as Defence Minister demonstrated, a strong man at the helm of the defence establishment guarantees civilian domination over the military in Israel. The lessons of 1954, and to some extent of 1967, have shown that the absence of a powerful defence minister supported by his government and people who can command the confidence of the high command, impedes the development of harmonious relationships between the two arms of national security in Israel, Zahal and the Ministry, and upsets their equilibrium, which in turn could impede political development in Israel.*

The Six Days' War also signalled the peril inherent in indecisive leadership. A garrisoned state under permanent threat of annihilation necessarily develops *unique* and special civil–military relationships. It would behove Israel's political élites to pay close attention to and define more clearly the role of the defence minister, which in practice was successfully institutionalized by Ben Gurion. The lesson of foreign experience, the practice generally accepted in the West of strictly separating civilian and military functions (which Lavon advocated after his resignation in 1955), has little validity for

---

* By contrast, the tragedy of the French military, but especially the high command, during the first half of the Third Republic was that it lost confidence in Republicanism and its unstable régimes. "For that reason", writes Ralston, "the entente between the army and the Republic, one of the cardinal features in the political development of France since 1871, has, temporarily at least, ended" (*The Army and the Republic*, 1967, p. 251).

I

Israel. It would not be wise for Israel's political parties, and especially its ruling party, Ma'i, or, for that matter, for any future government, to separate civil and military functions; to preserve the Ben Gurion legacy of combining premiership with the defence ministry in a powerful personality is to guarantee smooth and co-operative civil–military relations in Israel, and to guarantee the sustenance of powerful and politically autonomous political structures in Israel.

Zahal's officer corps is Israel's most cohesive professional group. The legacies of the past have been eradicated. Former Palmach and NMO officers intermingle and all are integrated and dedicated professional officers.[10] Governed by effective civilian institutions, the legacy of civilian supremacy under the leadership of a powerful defence minister who can inspire and direct the military establishment, the cohesiveness of Zahal officers and men, all of whom are Israeli-born and Zahal graduates dedicated to the values of the state and loyal to its government, has enhanced civilian control over the military because cohesiveness permits more effective control. In the absence of a Ben Gurion–Dayan charismatic type of leader, the equilibrium of civil–military relationships will again be strained. The attention of Israel's political élites should be focused on this institutional problem and on Dayan's formula for civil–military relations in Israel. It is our view that Israel's leading political party should pay attention and create formal and informal institutional procedures for the selection of the defence minister, and that these should be followed closely in the formation of future cabinets.

NOTES

1. We are not analysing the events that led up to the June war or its consequences for both Arabs and Israelis. The literature on this topic is continuously proliferating, and no single account can be regarded as positively authoritative for some time. The best assessment of the events which led to the war are found in Theodore Draper's "Israel and World Politics", *Commentary* (August 1967), pp. 19–59. Also, Bernard Lewis's essay, "The Arab–Israeli War: The Consequences of Defeat", *Foreign Affairs*, Vol. 46, No. 2 (January 1968), pp. 321–35. Respective Arab and Israeli arguments and interpretations are found in the respective press. See the Friday issue of *Al-Aharam*, especially Haykal's editorials, Nasser's speeches, and the Israeli dailies *Ha-Aretz*, *Ma-Ariv*, and *Yediot Aharonot* of the same period.

2. For complete details on the politics that led to the formation of a national unity cabinet and the appointment of General Dayan as Defence Minister, see S. Nakdimon, "The Drama that Preceded the Formation of the National Unity Government", *Yediot Aharonot* (Tel-Aviv) (October 18, 20, 25, 27, 1967); Shiff, "The Three Weeks that Preceded the War", *Ha-Aretz* (Tel-Aviv) (October 4, 1967), pp. 33–34, 43; the editors of Ma Ariv, "Interview with Prime Minister Levi Eshkol", *Ma-Ariv* (Tel-Aviv) (October 4, 1967), pp. 9–13. To corroborate the newspaper accounts, during the month of October 1967 in Israel, we interviewed members of the national unity cabinet (especially General Allon), members of parliament, and members of the high command of Zahal.

3. The issue was how did Western powers respond to Egypt's challenge to Israel. The Dayanists and General Allon claim that Eban misled the Premier with his over-optimism concerning the Johnson promise to break the blockade. Eban and his allies refute this, saying there was no misinterpretation of Eban's perception and understanding concerning the position of the United States, France, and Britain and other maritime powers. Obviously, in the absence of documentary evidence on either side, this issue must wait for the historians to resolve it. Raphael Bashan, "Interview with Eban", *Ma-Ariv* (March 22, 1968) and Bashan, "Interview with Allon", *Ma-Ariv* (April 12, 1968).

In the absence of available documents and in view of the inner political conflict among Israel's top leaders and the contradictory interpretations based on conflicting statements by public figures since June 1967 concerning the crucial decision to go to war during the month of May 1967 (and before that), it is left for serious scholars only to speculate on the complex decision-making process of that period in Israel. The literature on the decision to go to war is burgeoning. Again it is mainly of an apologetic nature. While Moshe Gilboa's *Shesh Shanim-Shishah Yamim (Six Years—Six Days)*, Am-Oved, Tel-Aviv, 1968, has been published in defence of Eshkol–Eban, Michael Bar Zohar's better journalistic effort, *Ha-Hodesh Ha-Aroch Beyoter (The Longest Month)*, Tel-Aviv, 1968, has been inspired by Rafi and vindicates its chiefs Ben Gurion–Dayan on Eshkol's defence gap. Both, however, were well briefed and were also privy to some documentation of their respective sponsors and therefore should be in the list of readings on the future analysis of the 1967 war. Except for Theodore Draper (mentioned earlier) and Laqueur's *The Road to Jerusalem*, Harper, 1968, most of the literature on the 1967 war in English, French and especially Hebrew is of an impoverished and sensational nature. It usually runs from lesser James Bond to campaign accounts (usually sloppy). The political-ideological literature is also proliferating; while on the one hand Israelis in most of the Western press and especially in *Ma-Ariv* and *Yediot Aharonot* are portrayed as supermen, the leftist press in Europe (France, Germany) and especially in the United States (most notably *Ramparts* and *Monthly Review*) have opted to champion the cause of the downtrodden Arabs oppressed by a variety of villains and imperialist augurs whose chief agent is Israel. It is needless to mention the character of this press. See a most incisive review and critique of the literature on the left and the 1967 war by M. S. Arnoni, "The Middle East and the Integrity of Some 'Analysts'," *The Minority of One*, Vol. 10, No. 6, June 1968, pp. 16–25. See also Robert Alter, "Israel and the Intellectuals", *Commentary*, Oct. 1967, pp. 46–52, and Martin Peretz, "The American Left and Israel", *Commentary*, Nov. 1967, pp. 27–34.

4. On the Mapai leadership's isolation from the people, see the un-

published study conducted by Professor Lissak, Department of Sociology of Hebrew University, "Social Mobility and Political Identity in the Israeli Society: Problems of Integration of Oriental Communities in the Social and Political Structure of Israel".

5. *Ramparts'* (July 1967) article on Dayan clearly demonstrated the magazine's own prejudices, and *Time* and *Newsweek*'s assessments of the man with the patch pleaded ignorance of the real Dayan.

6. "Interview with General Dayan", *Bamachane* (March 10, 1967), pp. 11–13; Rosenfeld, "Interview with Dayan", *Ma-Ariv* (April 30, 1968), p. 9.

7. See Janowitz, *Professional Soldier, op. cit.*, for a description of this type.

8. For security reasons their names could not be revealed before their appointments are made official in Israel on Independence Day, May 2, 1968.

9. It is expected that General Gavish, Bar-Lev's successor, will be the last Palmach veteran to become chief of staff. Bar-Lev's or Gavish's successor will be a Zahal graduate and probably a Dayanist.

10. An analysis (undertaken in another study) of social origins and attitudinal behaviour explains Zahal's internal organization, recruitment, and promotion policies. It could, as in the pre-independence era, *explain* the political expectations and behaviour of officers.

CHAPTER X

A Garrisoned State: The Israeli Solution

It would be pointless to pretend that Zahal's officer corps and especially its high command is in any simple sense a political group, for as a group it has no political aspirations other than those espoused by the people and the government of Israel. We hope to have marshalled enough evidence, however, to suggest that in defence and foreign affairs, Zahal's high command wields an enormous influence. This influence can be attributed to Israel's unusually precarious situation as a garrison-state, and to the special relations created by Ben Gurion's unchallenged domination of the defence establishment as demonstrated in the aftermath of the Lavon affair.

It may also be tempting to advance the argument that at times, especially during General Dayan's tenure as Commander-in-Chief, Zahal's high command has actually attempted to dominate Israel's foreign and defence policies, but the truth is precisely the opposite. As Defence Minister, Ben Gurion demanded that his chief aides share his convictions regarding Israel's defence posture. He especially chose men whom he could trust to successfully operationalize his security concepts. Ben Gurion also did not hesitate to "retire" before their time some of Israel's most capable senior officers, including three chiefs of staff, Generals Yadin, Makleff, and Laskov, when they sought greater independence for the military in security matters.[1]

Since its formation Israel, with its back to the sea, has depended on Zahal for its survival. The degree of Arab violence since 1936 increased geometrically to a point where Israel and its Arab neighbours by now are *mortal* enemies. The strength of Zahal is the difference between survival and annihilation for Israel. Thus the responsibility shouldered by Zahal and especially its chief of staff and on the high command is immense.

A defeat for Zahal could mean total destruction, since Egypt and the Arab nations are committed to the "liberation of Palestine"—in other words, the annihilation of Israel.* Israel has destroyed Arab armies several times and Arab nations continue to survive. The reversal is not true about Israel.

The identity between Zahal and the nation could not be more manifest than in times of supreme crisis when the loss of one means the destruction of the other. The defence minister and the chief of staff shoulder the heavy burden of the survival of this nation. The commander-in-chief of Zahal has been historically conscious of this fact. General Rabin counselled caution during the months of crisis, April–May 1967, aware of the immense military armament of Egypt. Here he has received *complete* support from the high command, also conscious of the onus of the *political* responsibilities on Zahal. Conscious of the tremendous burden imposed on him, Rabin (since Eshkol demonstrated irresolution) during the height of the crisis in 1967 (May 22–June 5) demanded resolution from his civilian chiefs. This occurred only when Dayan took over the office. Thus as chief military technocrat, Rabin could not act until his civilian chiefs, led by the defence minister, ordered Zahal to move on the Egyptian forces in Sinai.

It could be argued that another general (some say General Ezer Weizmann) could have persuaded the cabinet of the inevitability of war with Egypt once the Straits of Tiran were blocked. This is the function of the army as a branch of the government: to influence, persuade, and pressure the politicians to act as the professionals expect they should. This again only demonstrates that Zahal was in a position to persuade not to *dictate* the issue of war and peace in Israel. Ben Gurion's legacy as "head of war" was Rabin's iron law. That Eshkol fell short of his job and that chief of staff waited for political resolution to emerge from Eshkol's cabinet reiterates the *delicate* but *clear* separation of powers and functions that was institutionalized by the first defence minister of Israel. The practices and procedures of Ben Gurion and Dayan (the "hawks" in the view of inter-

---

* See the exhaustive and judicious study on the conflict by Yehoshafat Harkabi, *The Arab Position in the Israeli–Arab Conflict*, 1968, and also Amos Perlmutter, "Sources of Instability in the Middle East", ORBIS, Fall 1968. Vol. XII, No. 3, pp. 25–43.

national press and public opinion) clearly established the lines of political separation between civilian and military functions in Israel, as well as demonstrating their complexity in the case of Israel.

To argue that Dayan represents the so-called "military clique" is no more true than to claim that General Dwight D. Eisenhower, as President, represented the same. The "hard line" followed by Ben Gurion and Dayan does not reflect the will of any behind-the-scenes defence establishment; but rather the realities of a garrisoned state, and the sentiment of the Israeli electorate.[2] This added to the varied evidence presented in the course of this study leaves no grounds for the argument that Zahal's élite seeks to dominate the government, or that Zahal dictates the political, economic, and social destiny of Israel. For this to be true Zahal would have had to accomplish the following: the formulation and promotion of an alternative ideology; domination over economic policies; control of the process of modernization; and demonstration of its legitimacy through some form of autonomous political organization.

In other new nations, the army generally moves to power because it has lost confidence in the "corrupt politicians". That is, of course, conspicuously untrue in Israel, where Zahal's high command and its officer corps are loyal to civilian authorities. We know of no instance where Zahal's élite demonstrated lack of confidence in the Israeli political system, although as bureaucrats and citizens they may have doubted the efficacy and political wisdom of some of their leaders and the static nature of some structural mechanism in Israel's political system. The power of those who control Israel's army does not lie in the fact that they do control the army, but that they are dominant figures in the HOL and in the powerful Mapai party which have virtually run Israel since 1935. Thus, despite Ben Gurion's extraordinary personal influence he lost control over defence and the army when he formed the splinter party, Rafi. Levi Eshkol, the Defence Minister between 1965 and 1967, assumed full and *firm* control over Zahal, even if some officers privately did not regard his capabilities as Defence Minister very highly. General Dayan was appointed Defence Minister in the crisis of June 1967, not because he had great influence with Zahal, but because it was the will of the Israeli electorate.

The contest between military and civilian authorities thus was resolved in favour of the civilian. In fact, the conflict was clearly not based on a civilian–military rivalry for political supremacy. The factors underlying the rivalry were a consequence of the disequilibrium between voluntary and compulsory institutions, structures, practices, and procedures, created in the wake of Israel's political transformation.

The internal political struggle between civilian and military groups in the defence establishment was known to the cabinet and to the leadership of the HOL and Mapai, while the public remained inactive or passive. Only after 1960 did the public become active. Yet despite the fact that it became a public issue, the Lavon controversy was resolved in the Executives of the HOL, Mapai, and in the cabinet. The Lavon affair changed the nature of Mapai's internal coalition structure, giving weight to new groups, but did not enhance Zahal's influence over the party or the government.

Formalization and bureaucratization brought changes in the structure and activities of the traditional party and bureaucratic élites[3] and the formation of non-political élites, a rare phenomenon in the pre-independence era. Zahal is such a group. The whole spectrum of ideological commitment of officers, as was the case before 1948, has declined and in some areas has been eliminated.[4] One would venture the hypothesis that the political consciousness and ideological inclinations of Israel's junior officers (with the exception of junior officers who come from the left-oriented kibbutzim) is much lower than that of civil servants, legislators, and students.[5] But their career mobility is higher than any other social group in Israel (see Tables 4 and 5 in Chapter V, p. 63).

The political ambitions of the senior officers are also restricted. Only a few senior army officers have joined a political party (in fact, those who did join had been affiliated with a party before Zahal was established) and become active political figures, capitalizing on their war exploits and charismatic appeal; among them are Generals Dayan and Allon.

As veterans, Zahal's élite have played a key role in Israel's industrial and bureaucratic complex. Many have become prominent in the Israeli civil service, especially in the foreign service, and they play a key role in Israel's foreign assistance programmes in Africa and Latin America. The "smooth" integration of Zahal élite is crucial for civil–military relations in Israel. On the whole, the absorptive capacity of the Israeli society has been such that there has been no problem so far (this is due to the wide-ranging and disparate needs of the Israeli economy and bureaucratic structures).

Israel, in contrast to the other states in the Middle East—and to most newly emergent countries—is not a praetorian state.[6] A praetorian state is one in which the political system favours the development of the army as the central ruling group; a state in which the political leadership (as distinguished from bureaucratic, administrative, and managerial leadership) is mainly recruited from the army; a state, in short, in which the army serves as a reservoir for recruitment of political leaders. Among the conditions contributing to praetorianism are:

1. An ineffective and army-sustained political and civic culture. In Israel the civic culture has been long established and the persistence of the civilian over the military was successfully maintained in both the pre- and post-independence eras. Civilian supremacy has not been challenged since 1948—despite twenty years of security and border tensions, constant military preparedness, and three major wars.

2. A low level of political institutionalization and lack of sustained support for political structures.[7] Israel is one of the most politically complex and institutionally structured among the developing or newly developed states, demonstrating a high level of political institutionalization and sustained support of political structure and procedures.

3. Weak and ineffective political parties. In Israel, highly cohesive and stratified classes, groups, and political parties prevent the predominance of one faction over the others. Mapai and Histadrut are themselves confederations of interests, factions, and political cleavages.

4. Lack of common purpose and ideological consolidation. In Israel, practically no gap exists between the ideology of Zahal and that of the state or its major political parties. The universality and identity of values between civilian and military sectors makes a common effort inevitable. The army's role expansion is no more threatening to civilian supremacy than that of the Histadrut or Hityashvut systems. This does not mean

a total absence of constraints, but role expansion has been the legacy of Israel since the formation of the Yishuv.

5. Lack or decline of professionalism because political considerations win out over those of internal organization and career concerns. In Israel, professionalism and depoliticization have been on the rise. Zahal's depoliticization does not mean that the army could not serve as an avenue for attaining political leadership but only that the army's functions are not determined by the internal and parochial politics of labour or any other political organization. The officer corps could not become an ally of one political faction or another, as occurred in the Egyptian army before 1952, and is occurring in the Syrian and Iraqi armies today. The policy of depoliticization restrains the Israeli army and its officer corps from becoming a vehicle for political power.

The maturity of Israeli political structures, especially the highly complex and institutionalized political parties, the kibbutzim and the Histadrut, would present a formidable challenge to the army if it were to choose to play independent politics. The identification with the state of the most powerful and popular party, Mapai, and the kibbutz movement leaves no room for army officer manoeuvres of the sort which frequently occur in praetorian states. The army could not claim that the politicians had "betrayed" the nation. No civilian politicians, either as individuals or as organized groups, have meddled in the politics of the army since the dissolution of the Palmach and the NMO in 1948–1949. If some former military men, such as Generals Dayan and Allon, play a key role in Israeli politics today, it is only because they have resigned from the army and sought power *through* civilian political parties. The reputations they gained in the army may have enhanced the political chances of these prominent army commanders, but did not determine their political success. Any attempt on their part to influence politics while still in uniform would have been crushed with little effort. In fact, if military men desire to become successful politicians, they must channel these ambitions through civilian and political institutions and procedures.

Zahal has been a people's army and a reserve organization, its barracks life is short, the officers are permanently integrated with society, and the chances of the officers becoming ideologically or professionally independent are small.[8] A long military career in Israel is unlikely because the officer corps is being rotated continuously and thus is kept young, especially the "heroic" type. In view of this the chances for the alienation of the military from the body politic and the social system are non-existent.

Under present conditions, Israel's highly professionalized army, dependent on a reserve system, with a still unusually rapid turnover of officers and men, acts by virtue of its formal status and is harnessed to civilian control, as in the case of the non-garrisoned US and Western European armies. The officer corps as a professional group is removed, but is not isolated, from politics. Officers are prohibited from actively participating in politics and so far have shown little interest in politics after retirement. This again does not prevent the army élite from actively pressing for and seeking managerial, economic, and administrative positions.

It is not the *size* of the Israeli army and the enormous defence budget (during Sinai 18% of the total budget; now estimated at 40%) which dictates the political and attitudinal behaviour of the Israeli army and its high command.[9] Size and budget of armies are determining factors in praetorian states. In non-praetorian states, the army's size and the defence budget affect the economic structure which in turn may affect structural changes in society and politics but will not propel the army into the most prominent position as the political ruling group, as is the case in praetorian states. Nor does Israel fit the thesis that in a garrisoned state the army is prone to forgo the principle of professionalism or political non-intervention as was the case with the Prussian army from Bismarck to Hitler.[10] The values and the nationalist ideology of Zahal stem from the permanent Arab threat, and Zahal is committed to the nationalism espoused by most Israelis. In fact, the high command since 1967 is willing to underwrite a peace treaty with the Arabs based on secure and guaranteed borders, while a considerable section of the intelligentsia, journalists, and literary groups espouse Complete Israel—a policy advocating the absorption of 1967 occupied Arab territories. The army élite is differentiated from the social structure in a manner not unlike that of other élites; it is not a politically privileged group.

Thus, the rapid turnover of officers, the absorptive capacity of the economy, the economic and social integration of Zahal veterans, the nation's dependence upon the reserve system, the identity of political goals, and the army's professionalism, preclude Zahal's active intervention in politics. In addition, the institutionalized legitimacy of the independent civilian political structures furnish an effective guarantee of civilian control. The military in Israel—as a pressure group similar to those in other non-praetorian states where the civilian is formally and informally supreme—will nevertheless continue to challenge the civilian, especially in the realm of defence and foreign affairs.

NOTES

1. On the average, the tenure of Zahal's commanders-in-chief is three to five years. Yadin resigned after two years, Makleff after one year, and Laskov just after his third year of tenure had expired.

2. Our investigation into the reign of Eshkol as Defence Minister (1963–1967) leads us to conclude that Zahal has been aggrandized considerably during his reign as Minister. The high command has secured the best and most expensive weapons in Zahal's history. Even if this were due to a general development of weapons and to the Egyptian military build-up, Eshkol complied with most budgetary requests of the commanders-in-chief. In fact, when Ben Gurion served as Defence Minister, he encountered opposition from his Finance Minister Eshkol when requesting higher budgets for Zahal. Dayan recently admitted in person to some members of the high command that he intends to cut the "lavish" expenditures on defence. It is well known, for instance, that Ben Gurion opposed the 1967 war, mainly fearing Russian intervention and Israel's political isolation. Eshkol, on the other hand, who openly admits that he is no military expert accepted the advice of the army's chief intelligence officer, that the Soviets would not directly help the Egyptians.

3. Eisenstadt, *Israeli Society, op. cit.*, pp. 427–29.

4. The author is designing a study of the political ideology of the Israeli army's junior officers.

5. See Alan Arian, "Ideological Change in Israel: A Study of Legislators, Civil Servants, and University Students", unpub. diss., Department of Political Science, Michigan State University, 1965.

6. See author's "The Praetorian State and the Praetorian Army: Toward a Taxonomy of Civil–Military Relations in Developing Politics", *Comparative Politics*, April 1969 forthcoming.

7. See Samuel P. Huntington, "Political Development and Political Decay", *World Politics*, XVII (April 1965), and author's "Praetorianism", *op. cit.*, pp. 11–14.

8. Shiff, "The Young Officers of Zahal: Education and Political Consciousness", *Ha-Aretz* (September 18, 1963); see also Huntington, *The Soldier, op. cit.*, pp. 1–19.

9. See Andrzejewski, *Military Organization, op. cit.*, pp. 75–116.

10. See Huntington, *The Soldier, op. cit.*, especially type 4, p. 97.

The Military and Nation-Building:
Lessons for a Comparative Analysis

FOCUSING on the military as an instrument of nation-building in Israel is not to discount the large network of nation-building efforts and mobilization structures innovated by the Jewish pioneers in Palestine. In fact, as pointed out earlier, the military role in the pioneer settlement system was latent and meagre at first. If the year 1905 could be set as the start of Socialist-Zionist settlement in Palestine,[1] the Haganah did not become a serious occupation of the Yishuv until some thirty years later. The foundations for the creation of a new society and a new nation were laid and developed in a process of continuous and sustaining accumulation of social, economic, and political power, of which security and military functions were among several growing *along* and always in unison with the multi-purpose of the pioneer community. Thus the military, as an instrument of nation-building in Palestine, was a concomitant aspect in the creation of a pioneer settlement social and political system in Palestine. Since the creation of Israel in 1948, and the transformation of voluntary mobilizing economic and political structures into governmental bureaucracies, with the state and its machinery assuming all of the political functions and inheriting several of the socio-economic functions performed by the former, the army, now an instrument of the state, was delegated several functions previously performed by voluntary associations of the pioneer-settlement community.

The modal personality and image of the pioneer have been delegated to the officer: the pioneers' mobilizing values of leadership, egalitarianism, and vision were now institutionalized into Zahal, this in addition to Zahal's major function as a fighting unit. Clearly, the processes of institutionalization and of mobilization were different in Zahal than they were in the pre-1948 community. The most outstanding difference is that the military no longer serves a political interest, nor the ideology of exclusive groups—thereby relinquishing its former political autonomy. In performing its non-military functions, Zahal serves as an agent of the state, inculcating a nationalist consciousness and ideology into the army.

The lesson of the Israeli model for developing nations is that in Israel the army was *unified and nationalized prior* to most other political and economic functions and was made responsible to national authority as soon as the first cabinet was formed. In this way, the army could not become an instrument of any political party, special interests, or ambitious political and nationalist leaders. The rise of new nations is too often characterized by a military struggle against colonial powers where the army becomes predominant and its leaders naturally expect to become the nationalist leaders (true of some Latin-American polities and Algeria). This procedure was averted in Israel. The formalization and depoliticization of the army took place as soon as the struggle for independence was over. The persistence of Ben Gurion, in this respect, also guaranteed that, even under the most trying circumstances, the military could not develop an independent and autonomous political officer class. The opposite has been true in several developing nations which have emerged without a military struggle against colonial powers but, as the processes of nationalization and modernization broke down, witnessed the rise of the military as the guardian of society, the "revolution's" praetorian guard (in the Middle East, South-east Asia, and sub-Saharan Africa).

The task of inculcating the image and values of the pioneers imposed on the army several civic-action functions. This could be achieved without much difficulty since the nationalist ideology and values of Zahal and its officer corps converged with those of society. Since Zahal's role expansion does not threaten civilian rule, Israel ceases to serve as a model for several military élites in developing nations.

Military political action in developing polities takes place when the gap between élites and society is asymmetrical (Egypt) and the gap within the military élites (Syria) threatens the society with permanent military rule or in the case of the alienation of the military (Egypt) or its status deprivation (Chile and several Latin-American polities). In such cases, the military élite has easy access to power and could, and in several cases does, threaten the meagre fabric of civilian institutions. Also, in the absence of rival mobilizing political groups and structures which are cohesive and effective, the army in the end *dictates* the nationalist ideology and the purposes of society (Pakistan, Burma, Indonesia). Here military role expansion and reformist zeal, however desirable, could also threaten the development of autonomous and sustaining political structures, as is the case in Egypt, Syria, and several Middle Eastern and sub-Saharan African polities.

Although in Israel the army borrowed and inculcated the pioneer nationalist values of society, in several other developing nations the image of the military is inculcated into society. As simple nationalists or, as in several cases a former colonial satrap and/or ceremonial type, these officers and armies are not the most desirable models for nation-building, even if their civic action and political interventions are undertaken on behalf of principles and ideologies which were never the legacy or the tradition of the army. Israel's social values stem from society and not from the army; thus, in the area of army role expansion and civic action, Israel can serve only as a limited model for developing polities.

The Israeli influence on several African armies[2] and on the Burmese army[3] is well established by now. In Africa, especially, Israeli-type civic action is effective, but is restricted to the inculcation of youth culture[4] (Nahal type), since the army represents youth and thus revolutionary culture. Beyond this, the Israeli model could not serve African polities whose societal arrangements are asynchronist. In Africa, the soldier's legacy is British–French—characteristically conservative officers of the professional soldier type.[5]

A pattern has yet to emerge in Africa with regard to the nature of the norms established by the armed forces. Despite a long colonial history and a relatively short period of independence, the value systems of the military in former British colonies appear to be fairly harmonious with the traditional values of the society and are more African than European. There are, however, indications that the older officer groups (those commissioned prior to independence) and the transitional officer groups (those commissioned at or shortly after independence) tend to adhere to a value system which is imitative of European models. A good example is the case of Brigadier A. A. Afrifa, a member of the ruling National Liberation Council of Ghana, whose reminiscences of his days at Sandhurst reveal a profound acceptance of British institutions and values. He said of Sandhurst:

> It was a good, solid military school where one pulled one's self up as a man. I met many boys of my age for whom there was nothing sweeter than bearing arms in the service of their country, boys to whom Her Majesty's Army was a symbol of their very existence. . . . Sandhurst gave us independent thinking, tolerance, and a liberal outlook. . . . I loved the companionship of people of identical calling, and the English breakfast. . . . Now I look back on Sandhurst with nostalgia. It is one of the greatest institutions in the world.[6]

Expression of this nature would probably be more common among officers in French-speaking colonies whose adherence to the traditions of the French army prevailed even after their native countries became independent. Morris Janowitz[7] makes the distinction between ex-colonial and post-liberation armies and places both the former French and former British colonies in the latter category due to the lack of indigenous cadres prior to independence. It is problematical, however, whether both classes of states can comfortably fit into this category. The strong adherence to French values by African officers, manifested by their extensive intermarriage with French women and preferences for French culture and cuisine, indicate that even among the younger officers there is a significant rejection of traditional values in favour of imported ones and this results in the creation of a pseudo-French officer caste.

A contrary opinion is expressed in a book by William F. Gutteridge[8] who maintains that "the assumption that the military tradition in which . . . an élite is brought up determines its probable political and social behavior cannot be substantiated". Belmont Brice[9] states that, although African armies are not alienated from their societies, they are inherently separated from them to a degree that does not occur in Western societies. He attributes this not only to foreign influence but also to the level of educational and administrative expertise required to run a modern army. He does stress, however, the dependence of the new African states on foreign training and equipment as a factor in widening the gap between the soldier and society and that the gap between political modernization and African leaders' expectations widens and paves the way for the more pragmatic leaders, the military, to move in. Zolberg clearly demonstrates that the gap is not only between the various élites of modernization in the case of several Sab-Saharan polities but between the centre and the periphery where the army could represent either but on the whole represents the centre.[10]

In Latin-America during the 19th century, the considerable gap between the officer corps and the people was determined as much by social and economic class distinctions as by the army's acceptance of imported values. Germani and Silvert, however, point out that in Latin-America it was the creole élite who masterminded the revolutions, rather than the resident native Spaniards and Portuguese, and that the revolutions were supported by the Negro, Indian, and Mestizo soldiers.[11] Accordingly, although the officer corps was separated from the mass of society by birth, position, and status, nevertheless, it was an indigenous group adept at manipulating national symbols consistent with those recognized by most individuals in the society. This was true of the Khedive's army in Egypt and was manifest in Colonel Ahmad Arabi revolt (1881).[12]

Certain aspects of Israeli-style military role expansion and civic action could be adapted successfully for use by developed polities, such as the United States. Youth culture, civic values, ethnic integration, and societal mobilization could be assigned to the American army. Although a military domestic peace corps would probably be unpopular in a society bitterly divided on Vietnam and on racial issues, it would not prevent the Vietnam veteran or Negro officer from playing an important role in the Negro ghetto. He could serve as a model of the heroic type, a leader of a youth culture, as does the Israeli officer with the new immigrant recruit. The subculture values of the Negro officer and the Negro ghetto are not as disparate as that of White from Negro subcultures. The American army "until

K

recent times one of America's most segregated institutions, has leaped into the forefront of racial equality in the past decade".[12]

The most important lesson to be drawn from the Israeli experience is the use of the army as an effective and successful instrument for modernization and nation-building. Kemalist Turkey[13] has also demonstrated that an army can be used successfully as a nation-builder; however, in the majority of new nations, it is dubious if similarly effective results could be obtained.

The Israeli experience brings to mind several questions with regard to civil–military relations in complex and highly developed political systems. The complexity of those relationships, in a technological and nuclear age, has been successfully analysed by Morris Janowitz,[14] especially with regard to changing organizational authority;[15] narrowing the differential between military and civilian élites;[16] the rate of technological change; diversification and specialization of military technology;[17] and the complexity of the machinery of warfare. All of these factors contribute to the "civilianization" of the military, and social scientists are gradually coming to regard the military as a legitimate social system.[18]

As a highly developed social system, Zahal established intricate and complex relationships with Israeli society on a personal, ideological, and institutional level. The army of Israel is a true profile of its society. The emergence of personal alliances[19] between civilian and military élites in Israel goes back to the beginnings of the pioneer settlement movement in Palestine. The Hashomer, the Haganah, the Labour Legion, the UKM, the Palmach, the NMO, and its factions, demonstrate a concomitant and simultaneous growth of these alliances.

Recent events in Syria illustrate the opposite of the Israeli experience. The simultaneous emergence of a radical wing, the Ba'th Party, and a politically oriented group of army officers has enhanced divisiveness and personalism in both groups and encouraged the political ambitions of individual officers. In the absence of group cohesion, neither group can prevail, although the military precariously dominates the Ba'th Party. The major reason for the relative political stability in Syria since the February 1966 coup is that the army is now dominated by

Alawi officers who are buttressed by Alawi social and kinship systems.[20]

The characteristics of these alliances in Israel are the cohesivity of military and civilian groups and the organizational, ideological, and political predominance of the latter. Although civil and security organizations grew simultaneously, the former always guided and dominates the latter. In the pre-independence era, military structures were sometimes viewed as a political instrument of the former and to embody this or that group's conception or vision of nation-building. The equilibrium between civilian and military institutions in Israel was reached only after the nationalization of Zahal. Yet personal alliances between civilian and military élites persist (see Table 9 in Chapter VI, p. 77). The chances of professional rigidity and the emergence of a professional soldier isolated from the societal, political, and ethical fabric of Israel were successfully averted, in part by Ben Gurion's conscious policy of encouraging the development of close relations between civilians and the military in the defence establishment.

Societal isolation of an officer class threatens working relationships between civilian and military élites. To prevent this, Israel's army has worked out a system which facilitates the transition from soldier to civilian and makes it relatively easy for yesterday's client of the army to become today's client of the party, bureaucracy, or industry of his choosing.

The creation of interlocking relationships between the military and civilian functions of defence did not pose a danger as some critics of the Ministry argued. It was Lavon's attempt to separate them which precipitated the only major crisis in civil–military relationships since independence. The interdependence between the "head of war" and the chief of staff is crucial in Israel. This was clearly understood by Dayan and Rabin in relation to the minister of defence.

The effectiveness of the military as a pressure group in the United States depends upon the creation of a network of civilian alliances;[21] this could also be said of the Israeli high command. However, it could equally be said that civil–military alliances in Israel contribute to the effectiveness of the civilians who run the defence establishment. Ben Gurion's charismatic influence and Dayan's domineering personality have also enhanced their control and influence over the military. The relatively short military career open to Zahal officers militates against the formation of a rigid and conservative professional *Weltanschauung*, which is characteristic of men who make the army a lifetime vocation. This, of course, does not mean that the military mind is not found in Zahal, but his career pattern does not permit him much headway.

The ability of the defence minister (as was the case with Ben Gurion and is expected of Dayan) to fuse civil–military élites and to shoulder the political responsibility for military actions has shaped the pattern of civil–military relations in Israel. In the periods where military and political élites were separate and diffuse, either due to personalist ambitions of the defence minister (Lavon) or to his non-expertise (Eshkol), the army's effectiveness as a political pressure group was enhanced. But its efficiency was threatened by political irresolution. The fusing of civilian and military élites reinforces the nation's pioneer-democratic ideals. In Israel, the heroic officer type, so often a threat to democratic values in other nations, actually serves to institutionalize them. The role expectation of this type of officer is patterned after the image of the Palmach. In Syria the heroic officer performs the opposite function by supporting the anti-democratic ideals of the PPS or Ba'th Party. He is usually a permanent coup-maker, a fanatical desperado bound by the rigid mumbo-jumbo and political messianism of his party.[22]

A strong civilian leadership over the defence establishment imbued with political daring and resolution—if this civilian leadership is dedicated to social-democratic values—guarantees the diffusion of these values into the army.[23] On the basis of the last two decades, and in view of the challenge during the Lavon reign, we cannot foresee a drastic turn of events, when the military would no longer be dedicated to these values.

In the absence of a minister who resolves to undertake the Clausewitzian doctrine on the unity of military and politics with the predominance of the latter, the former will naturally assert itself. Ben Gurion's vision of the defence minister as the "head of war" contributed to the preservation, subordination, and efficiency of the military.

The lessons of the past two decades teach that military

adventures can lead to disaster and that military victories, unexploited by political wisdom, are in themselves a wasteful and futile effort.

The challenge that confronts General Moshe Dayan, Ben Gurion's disciple and heir, is to prove that as a civilian "head of war" in a garrisoned state, he can exploit the 1967 victories to establish an Arab–Israeli *rapprochement* and prove that the civilian predominance over the military is the nation's best guarantee. The conduct of the new minister will be tested by his ability to clearly demonstrate that he has an understanding of the Clausewitzian dictum.

NOTES

1. We purposely omit the *Bilu* and agrarian settlements between 1875 and 1905, since this type of settlement did not take hold in Palestine, except for a few Moshavot.

2. Leopold Laufer, *Israel and the Developing Countries: New Approaches to Cooperation* (New York: Twentieth Century Fund, 1967), pp. 30–31, 167–72. Mandedrai Kreinin, *Israel and Africa—A Study in Technical Cooperation* (New York: Praeger, 1904). See also Oron, *MER 1960, op. cit.*, pp. 302–06, and *MER 1961, op. cit.*, pp. 329–47.

3. See Lissak, "Modernization", *op. cit.*, pp. 235–37.

4. On Nahal see Heymount, "Israeli Nahal Program", *op. cit.*, pp. 314–24; Laufer, *Israel, op. cit.*, pp. 30–31, 167–70; Oron, *MER 1961, op. cit.*, pp. 329–47.

5. On the professional soldier's conservative military mind, see Huntington, *The Soldier, op. cit.*, pp. 93–94.

6. A. A. Afrifa, *The Ghana Coup, 29th February 1966* (London: Frank Cass & Co. Ltd., 1966), pp. 50–51.

7. Janowitz, *The Military in the Political Development of New Nations* (Chicago: University of Chicago Press, 1964), p. 15.

8. William F. Gutteridge, *Military Institutions and Power in the New States* (New York: Praeger, 1965), pp. 115–16.

9. Belmont Brice, "The Military in Subsaharan Africa", *African Forum* (Summer 1966), p. 59.

10. Aristide Zolberg, "Military Rule and Political Development in Tropical Africa", unpublished working paper ISA meeting, London, September 1967, pp. 1–3. Also Zolberg, *Creating Political Order*, Rand McNally, Chicago, 1966, pp. 9–36, 151–61.

11. Gino Germani and Kalman H. Silvert, "Politics, Social Structure and Military Intervention in Latin America", in Wilson C. McWilliams (ed.), *Garrisons and Governments* (San Francisco: Chandler, 1967), p. 230.

12. Morroe Berger, *Military Elite and Social Change; Egypt Since Napoleon* (Princeton: Center for International Studies, Princeton University, 1960), pp. 12–16.

13. Charles C. Moskos, "Racial Integration in the Armed Forces", *American Journal of Sociology*, Vol. 72, No. 2 (September 1966), p. 147.

14. On Turkey see Dankwart A. Rustow, "The Military in Middle

Eastern Society and Politics", in S. N. Fisher (ed.), *The Military*, pp. 3–20; W. F. Weiker, *The Turkish Revolution 1960–1961: Aspects of Military Politics* (Washington: Brookings Institution, 1963); George Antonius, *Arab Awakening, op. cit.*; Rustow, "The Army and the Founding of the Turkish Republic", *World Politics*, XI (October 1959), pp. 513–52; Kemal Karpat, *Turkey's Politics; The Transition to a Multi-Party System* (Princeton: Princeton University Press, 1959); and Daniel Lerner and Richard D. Robinson, "Swords and Ploughshares: The Turkish Army as a Modernizing Force", *World Politics*, Vol. 31 (October 1960), pp. 19–44.

15. Janowitz, *Professional Soldier, op. cit.*, pp. 8–15.

16. Janowitz, "Changing Patterns of Organizational Authority: The Military Establishment", *Administrative Science Quarterly*, Vol. 3 (March 1959), pp. 473–93.

17. Janowitz, *Professional Soldier*, pp. 9–10.

18. Janowitz, *The New Military: Changing Patterns of Organization* (New York: Russell Sage Foundation, 1964).

19. Janowitz and Little, *Sociology*, pp. 9–26.

20. On personal alliances in different context see Janowitz, *Professional Soldier, op. cit.*, pp. 291–301.

21. See Amos Perlmutter, "From Opposition to Rule: The Syrian Army and the Ba'th Party", *Western Political Quarterly* (forthcoming). From a burgeoning of literature of this topic, we recommend Patrick Seale, *The Struggle for Syria: A Study of Post-War Arab Politics 1945–1958* (London: Oxford University Press, 1965); Malcolm Kerr, *The Arab Cold War 1958–1967* (Oxford, 2nd ed., 1967); Eliezer Beeri, *Military and Society in the Arab East* (Heb.) (Tel-Aviv: Sifriat Poalim, 1966). Avraham Ben-Tzur, "The Neo-Bath Party of Syria", *Journal of Contemporary History*, Vol. 3, No. 3, 1968, pp. 161–82. Also Amos Perlmutter, "Arab Armies in Politics", Institute of International Studies, University of California at Berkeley, 1966 (mimeo).

22. Janowitz, *Professional Soldier, op. cit.*, p. 372.

23. See Seale, *The Struggle, op. cit.*, pp. 38–39.

24. One could not speculate what the relationship would be between Zahal and a government dominated by the left or the right. In any case either extreme could not form a coalition government short of a moderate-centrist alliance.

GLOSSARY

Ahdut Ha-Avoda—United Labour Party. Formed as a coalition of Poale Zion and other minor Socialist-Zionist parties in Eretz Israel in 1919. Joined Histadrut in 1920. Merged with Hapoel Hatzair in 1929 to form the Mapai party. Faction B, which split from Mapai in 1942, assumed the old name Ahdut Ha-Avoda. In 1954, when split from Mapam, this group assumed the name Ha-Tnu'ah Le-Ahdut ha-Avoda.

Aliyah—(pl. Aliyot) Immigration.

Aman—Zahal's Intelligence Branch.

Bedek—Israel's air industry; run by the Defence Ministry.

Beitar—Abbreviation for Brit Yoseph Trumpeldor, unity of Y. Trumpeldor's Revisionist youth movement.

Fidayun—Egyptian organized guerrilla. Under Egyptian armed control. Established in 1955 launching raids from the Gaza Strip (then under Egyptian occupation).

Gadna—Haganah's and Zahal's youth paramilitary troops.

Gahal—Electoral alignment of General Zionist and Herut parties since the 1965 elections.

Gdud Ha-Avoda—Labour Legion. Established by Yoseph Trumpeldor in 1920 to aid the growth of pioneer settlements; played a decisive role in the creation of Ha-Kibbutz ha-Meuchad.

Gdudim—Legions.

Ha-'Apala—Illegal immigration. The organization of the exodus of Jews to Israel.

Haganah—Defence. Jewish underground in Palestine, led and organized by the labour movement. As an organization, begun in 1921.

Ha-Esek ha-Bish—Israeli spyring in Egypt; the 1954 Fiasco. See note on pp. 000–000, Chapter VII.

Ha-Kibbutz ha-Artzi—National kibbutz. Hashomer Hatzair's kibbutz bloc. Established in 1927.

Ha-Kibbutz ha-Meuchad—United Kibbutz. One of Israel's influential kibbutzim blocs established in 1927 in Ein Harod. Played a key role in the history of Haganah and Palmach.

Ha-Koach He-hadash—Ben Gurion's faction in the Mapai party conference in February 1965. In August 1965 split from Mapai to make Rafi.

Ha-Mosad—The Institute. Haganah and Israel's special intelligence services.

Ha-Nodedet—The Patrol. Sadeh's and Wingate's defence outfit, recruited from Hityashvut youth to defend the settlements. Also known as Mishmar Na' (Moving Guards).

Hapoel Hatzair—The young labourer. The Palestinian Socialist-Zionist party, non-Marxist, founded in 1905 in Petah Tiqvah. Merged with Ahdut Ha-Avoda in 1929 to make the Mapai party.

Hashomer—The watchman. Jewish self-protection organization. Established in 1909.

Havlagah—Containment. The passivist resistance policy advocated by moderate elements in Zionism and by the Yishuv.

Hehalutz—The pioneer. The movement of pioneers for Palestine. Founded by Yoseph Trumpeldor in 1918.

Hemed—(Heil Mada') Zahal's scientific branch.

Herut—Freedom party. A Revisionist party, legal successor, since 1948, to NMO; led by Menahem Begin, former commander of NMO.

Hevrat Ovdim—Workers' Society. Histadrut's Central Economic and enterprises authority established in 1927.

Hish—Haganah's paramilitary organization in the cities.

Histadrut—Literally, "organization". The General Federation of Jewish Labour in Eretz Israel, founded in 1921.

Hityashvut—Settlement. Reference to pioneer agrarian settlement.

Homa U-migdal—Fortress and tower, defence settlement system during the 1936–1939 Arab Revolt.

Irgun Zvai Leumi—National Military Organization (NMO) founded by David Raziel and Avraham Stern of the Revisionist party in 1938. Between 1944–1948 led by Menahem Begin.

Kevishim—Roads.

Kibbutz—(pl. Kibbutzim) Collective; an organization of workers on a communal basis.

Knesset—Israeli Parliament; established 1949.

Lehi—(Lochame Herut Israel) Israel Freedom Fighters, a Revisionist underground movement engaged in personal terrorism, established by Stern in 1940. After his assassination, led by Natan Friedman-Yellin. This group was dissolved at the Second Knesset elections in 1951.

Ma'arach—The Alignment; the parliamentary party and electoral alliance of Mapai and Ahdut Ha-Avoda formed in 1965.

Maavak—Resistance.

Mafdal—Abbreviation for Miflagah Datit Leumit (National

Religious Party); since 1948 in coalition with Mapai. Played a key role in the appointment of Dayan as Defence Minister in 1967.

Ma'i—Israel Labour Party, formed in 1968. The alliance of Ahdut Ha-Avoda, Mapai, and Rafi.

Makabi—Jewish international and an Israeli sports movement, affiliated with bourgeois Zionism.

Mamlachtiout—See footnote 11, Chapter V, pp. 67–68.

Mapai—Abbreviation for Mifleget Poale Eretz Israel (Israel's Labour Party), formed when Hapoel Hatzair united with Ahdut Ha-Avoda in 1929. Social-democratic in its orientation.

Mapam—Abbreviation for Mifleget Poalim Meuchedet (United Labour Party), formed when Hashomer Hatzair united with Ha-Tnu'ah Le-Ahdut ha-Avoda in 1948. Marxist in orientation.

Moshav—Small holders co-operative settlement.

Moshava—A privately owned agricultural settlement.

Mem-mem—Platoon commanders; Palmach's nucleus force.

NMO—(National Military Organization). Abbreviation for all splinters of Zionist Revionist military structures.

Nahal—(Noar Halutzi Lohem) Fighting Youth Movement. Zahal's special military–agricultural pioneer unit; established in 1949.

Notrim—Agricultural settlement guards; Haganah's first legal army; established by British to protect Jewish settlement against Arab terrorism during the Arab revolt between 1936 and 1939.

Palmach—Abbreviation for Plugot Ha-Machatz; Haganah's Shock Platoons; established in 1941, these served as the élite of Haganah. They were dissolved in 1949 when Zahal was organized into the army of the State of Israel.

Poale Zion—Workers of Zion. The first Socialist–Zionist party in the Diaspora. Poale Zion groups were scattered without any organizational unity in different Russian towns around the early days of the century. Borochov's group was formed in 1901. Marxist in orientation. Palestinian Poale Zion group was formed in 1906 in Ramleh. Poale Zion still operates in the United States, Canada and many other Western European countries.

Rafi—Mapai splinter group, 1965. The Ben Gurion–Dayan–Peres faction. Dissolved in 1968 and joined Maarach (The Alignment) to make Ma'i Israel Labour Party in 1968.

Rechesh—Purchase; Haganah's clandestine weapon-purchasing organization.

Revisionist Party—Vladimir Jabotinsky's splinter group from the WZM. An extreme nationalistic party whose platform calls for the annexation of the Eastern Jordan territory. Founded in 1925 in Paris; formed the New Zionist Organization in 1933.

Shay—(Sherut Yediot) Haganah's political intelligence service Part of Ha-Mosad.

Siya Bet—Faction B, Mapai's opposition, organized in the middle 1930s; split from Mapai to form Ha-Tnu'ah Le-Ahdut ha-Avoda in 1944.

Ta'as—Haganah's and Israel's munitions industry; run by the Defence Ministry.

Yishuv—Community, settlement. Up to the second immigration wave Yishuv refers to the baronial farmer settlement, antagonistic to Zionism and to the Zionist-Socialists. Since the change in Palestine with the increase of Zionist aliyot, the term applies to the growing constructive Zionist community in Eretz Israel.

Zahal—Israel Defence Forces; abbreviation for Zva Ha-Haganah Le-Israel. Established under the Defence Service Act of March 1949.

BIBLIOGRAPHY

BOOKS IN FOREIGN LANGUAGES

Abcarius, M. F. *Palestine Through the Fog of Propaganda*. London: 1946.

Afrifa, A. A. *The Ghana Coup, 29th February 1966*. London: Frank Cass & Co. Ltd.

Andrzejewski (now Andreski), Stanislaw. *Military Organization and Society*. London: Routledge & Kegan Paul, 1954.

Antonius, George. *The Arab Awakening*. New York: Capricorn Books, 1965.

Bar-Zohar, Michael. *Suez Ultra-Secret*. Paris: Fayard, 1964.

Begin, Menahem. *The Revolt*. (Tr. Samuel Katz; ed. Ivan M. Greenberg.) New York: Henry Schuman, 1951.

Bendix, Reinhard. *Max Weber: An Intellectual Portrait*. Garden City: Doubleday, 1960.

Ben Gurion, David. *Rebirth and Destiny of Israel*. (Ed. and tr. Mordekhai Nurock.) New York: Philosophical Library, 1954.

—— *Selections*. New York: Labor Zionist Organization of America, Poale Zion, 1948.

Berger, Earl. *The Covenant and the Sword: Arab–Israeli Relations 1948–56*. London: Routledge & Kegan Paul, 1965.

Berger, Morroe. *Military Elite and Social Change; Egypt Since Napoleon*. Princeton: Center of International Studies, Princeton University, 1960.

Burns, E. L. M. *Between Arab and Israeli*. New York: Ivan O. Bolensky, 1963.

Burstein, Moshe. *Self-Government of the Jews in Palestine since 1900*. Tel-Aviv: Hapoel Hatzair, 1934.

Challener, R. D. *The French Theory of the Nation in Arms, 1866–1939*. New York: Columbia University Press, 1955.

Craig, Gordon. *The Politics of the Prussian Army 1640–1945*. New York, Oxford 1956.

Dayan, Moshe. *Diary of the Sinai Campaign*. London: Weidenfeld & Nicolson, 1966.

Eisenstadt, S. N. *Essays on the Sociological Aspects of Political and Economic Development*. The Hague: Mouton & Co., 1960.

—— *The Absorption of Immigrants*. London: Routledge & Kegan Paul, 1954.

—— *Israeli Society*. New York: Basic Books, 1968.

Esco Foundation for Palestine. *Palestine: A Study of Jewish, Arab, and British Policies*. 2 vols. New Haven: Yale University Press, 1947.

Etzioni, Amitai. *The Active Society*. New York: The Free Press, 1968.

Eytan, Walter. *The First Ten Years: A Diplomatic History of Israel*. New York: Simon & Schuster, 1958.

Fein, Leonard. *Israel*. Boston: Little, Brown, 1967.

Finer, Samuel. *Man on Horseback*. New York: Praeger, 1962.

Fischoff, Ephraim. *The Sociology of Religion*. Boston: Beacon Press, 1963.

Fisher, S. N. (ed.). *The Military in the Middle East*. Columbus: Ohio State University Press, 1963.

Gerth, Hans S., and C. Wright Mills (trs.). *From Max Weber: Essays in Sociology*. New York: Oxford University Press, 1946.

Goerlitz, Walter. *The German General Staff 1657–1945*. New York: Praeger, 1953.

Gutteridge, William F. *Military Institutions and Power in the New States*. New York: Praeger, 1965.

Halpern, Ben. *The Idea of the Jewish State*. Cambridge: Harvard University Press, 1961.

Hanna, Paul L. *British Policy in Palestine*. Washington: American Council on Public Affairs, 1942.

Huntington, Samuel P. (ed.). *Changing Patterns of Military Politics*. New York: The Free Press, 1962.

—— *The Soldier and the State*. New York: Vintage, 1964.

Hurewitz, J. C. *Diplomacy in the Near and Middle East*. Vol. I, 1535–1914; Vol. II, 1914–1956. New York: Van Nostrand, 1956.

—— *The Struggle for Palestine*. New York: W. W. Norton, 1950.

Janowitz, Morris. *The Military in the Political Development of New Nations*. Chicago: University of Chicago Press, 1964.

—— *The New Military: Changing Patterns of Organization*. New York: Russell Sage Foundation, 1964.

—— *The Professional Soldier*. New York: The Free Press, 1960.

—— and Roger Little. *Sociology and the Military Establishment*. Rev. ed. New York: Russell Sage Foundation, 1965.

Johnson, John J. (ed.). *The Role of the Military in Underdeveloped Countries*. Princeton: Princeton University Press, 1962.

Joseph (Yoseph), Bernard. *British Rule in Palestine*. Washington: Public Affairs Office, 1948.

Karpat, Kemal. *Turkey's Politics; The Transition to a Multi-Party System*. Princeton: Princeton University Press, 1959.

Katznelson, Berl. *Revolutionary Constructivism*. New York: Young Poale Zion Alliance, 1937.

Kerr, Malcolm. *The Arab Cold War 1958–1967*. London: Oxford University Press, 2nd ed., 1967.

Kreinin, Mordechai. *Israel and Africa—A Study in Technical Cooperation*. New York: Praeger, 1964.

Laufer, Leopold. *Israel and the Developing Countries: New Approaches to Cooperation*. New York: Twentieth Century Fund, 1967.

Lorch, Natanel. *The Edge of the Sword: Israel's War of Independence 1947–1949*. New York: Putnam's, 1961.

Marshall, S. L. A. *Sinai Victory*. New York: Morrow, 1958.

McWilliams, Wilson C. (ed.). *Garrisons and Governments*. San Francisco: Chandler, 1967.

Mosca, Gaetano. *The Ruling Class*. (Ed. Arthur Livingston) New York: McGraw-Hill, 1939.

Nettl, T. P. *Political Mobilization: A Sociological Analysis of Methods and Concepts.* London: Faber & Faber, 1967.

Oron, I. (ed.). *Middle East Record 1960.* London: Weidenfeld & Nicolson, 1962.

—— (ed.). *Miidle East Record 1961.* Tel-Aviv: Israel Oriental Society, 1967.

Patterson, John H. *With the Judeans in the Palestinian Campaign.* London: 1922.

Pearlman, Moshe. *The Army of Israel.* New York: Philosophical Library, 1950.

Rose, Harold M. (ed.). *The Institutions of Advanced Societies.* Minneapolis: University of Minnesota Press, 1958.

Safran, Nadav. *The United States and Israel.* Cambridge: Harvard University Press, 1963.

Schechtman, Joseph B. *Rebel and Statesman.* 3 vols. New York: Thomas Yoseloff, 1956.

Seale, Patrick. *The Struggle for Syria: A Study of Post-War Arab Politics 1945–1958.* London: Oxford University Press, 1965.

Seligman, L. G. *Leadership in a New Nation: Political Development in Israel.* New York: Atherton Press, 1964.

The Six Days' War. Israel Ministry of Defence, 1967.

Sykes, Christopher. *Orde Wingate.* Cleveland, Ohio: World Publishers, 1959.

Vagts, A. *History of Militarism.* 2nd ed. Meridan, 1954.

Weber, Marianne. *Max Weber.* Heidelberg: L. Scheider, 1960.

Weber, Max. *The Theory of Social and Economic Organization.* (Trs. A. M. Henderson and Talcott Parsons.) New York: Oxford University Press, 1947.

Weiker, W. F. *The Turkish Revolution 1960–1961: Aspects of Military Politics.* Washington: Brookings Institution, 1963.

Weizmann, Chaim. *Trial and Error: An Autobiography.* New York: Harpers, 1949.

Zeine, Zeine N. *Arab–Turkish Relations and the Emergence of Arab Nationalism.* Beirut: Khayats', 1958.

BOOKS IN HEBREW

Ahdut Ha-Avoda. *Yalkut Ahdut Ha-Avoda: (Ahdut Ha-Avoda Anthology).* 2 vols. Tel-Aviv: Ahdut Ha-Avoda, 1929.

Allon, Yigal. *Masach Shell Hol (Curtain of Sand).* Tel-Aviv: Ha-Kibbutz ha-Meuchad, 1960.

Arieli, Y. *Ha-Kenunya (The Intrigue).* Tel-Aviv: Kadima, 1965.

Arlozoroff, Chaim. *Jerusalem Diary.* Tel-Aviv: Mapai, 1932.

Assaf, Michael. *The Arab Awakening and their Departure.* Tel-Aviv: Davar, 1967.

Avigur, Shaul. *'Im Dor Ha-Haganah (The Haganah Generation).* Tel-Aviv: Ma'arachot, 1962.

Banai, Ya'aqov. *Hayalim Almonim (Unknown Soldiers).* Tel-Aviv: Hug Yedidim, 1958.

Bar-Zohar, Michael. *Gesher 'al Ha-yam ha-tichon* (*A Bridge over the Mediterranean Sea*). Tel-Aviv: Am Hasepher, 1963.

—— *Ha-Hodesh Ha-Aroch Beyoter* (*The Longest Month*). Am Hasepher, Tel-Aviv, 1968.

Basok, Moshe (ed.). *The Book of Hehalutz*. Jerusalem: The Jewish Agency, 1940.

Bauer, Yeduda. *Diplomatiya Ve-Mahteret* (*Diplomacy and Underground in Zionism 1939–1945*). Merhavia: Sifriat Poalim, 1966.

Beer, Israel. *Bitahon Israel* (*Israel's Security*). Tel-aviv: Amikam, 1966.

Beeri, Eliezer. *Military and Society in the Arab East*. Tel-Aviv: Sifriat Poalim, 1966.

Ben Gurion, David. *Ba-Ma'aracha* (*In the Battle*). 5 vols. Tel-Aviv: Ayanot, 1947–1955.

—— *Devarim Kehavayatam* (*Things as They Are*). Tel-Aviv: Am Hasepher, 1965.

—— *Ketavim* (*Works*). 4 vols. Tel-Aviv: Mapai, 1949.

—— *Ma'arechet Sinay* (*The Sinai Campaign*). Tel-Aviv: Am Oved, 1959.

—— *Mema'amad le-Am* (*From Class to Nation*). Tel-Aviv: Ayanot, 1954.

—— *Pegishot 'im Manhigim 'Aravim* (*Talks with Arab Leaders*). Tel-Aviv: Am Oved, 1967.

Braslavsky, Moshe. *Tnuat Ha-Poalim Ha-Eretz Israelit* (*The Palestine Labour Movement*). Tel-Aviv: Ha-Kibbutz ha-Meuchad, 1955–1956.

Dinour, Ben Zion, et al. (eds.). *Sepher Toldot Ha-Haganah* (*The History of the Haganah*). Vol. I, Part I, 1954, Part II, 1956; Vol. II, Part I, 1959, Part II, 1964, Part III, 1964. Tel-Aviv: Ma'arachot.

Dror, Levi, and I. Rosenzweig (eds.). *Sepher Hashomer Hatzair* (*Hashomer Hatzair Book*). Vol. I, 1913–1945. Merhavia: Sifriat Poalim, 1956.

Eisenstadt, S. N., H. Adler, R. Bar-Yosef, and R. Kahane. *The Social Structure of Israel*. Jerusalem: Akademon, 1966.

"Eretz Israel", *Encyclopedia Hebraica*. Tel-Aviv: Massada, 1957. Vol. 6.

Evron, Yoseph, *Beyom Sagrir* (*The Cold Years*), Tel-Aviv, Otpaz, 1968.

Friedman-Yellin, Natan and Israel Eldad (eds.). *The History of Lehi*. 2 vols. Tel-Aviv: Private pub., 1962.

Gdud Ha-Avoda. *Kovetz Gdud Ha-Avoda* (*Labour Legion Collection*). Tel-Aviv: Gdud Ha-Avoda, 1932.

Gilboa, Moshe. *Shesh-Shanim Shishah Yamim* (*Six Years—Six Days*). Tel-Aviv: Am-Oved, 1968.

Gilad, Zrubavel (ed.). *Magen Ba-Seter* (*Hidden Shield: The Secret Military Effort of the Yishuv during the War, 1939–1945*). Jerusalem: Jewish Agency, 1951.

—— (ed.). *Sepher Ha-Palmach* (*The Book of Palmach*). 2 vols. Tel-Aviv: Ha-Kibbutz ha-Meuchad, 1955.

Golomb, Eliahu. *Hevion Oz* (*Secret of Strength*). Tel-Aviv: Haganah, 1944.

Habas, Bracha, and Eliezer Schochet. *Sepher Ha-Aliya Ha-Shnia* (*The Book of the Second Immigration*) Tel-Aviv: Am Oved, 1947

Harkabi, Yehoshafat, *Emdat Ha-Aravim B'Sikhsukh Yisrael-Arav* (*The Arab Position in the Israel–Arab Conflict*). Tel-Aviv: Dvir, 1968.

Hasin, E., and D. Horwitz. *The Affair*. Tel-Aviv: Am Hasepher, 1961.

Historical Branch of Zahal. *Toldot Milhemet Ha-Komemiout* (*History of the War of Liberation*). (Preface by David Ben Gurion.) Tel-Aviv: Ma'arachot, 1959.

Katz, Shmuel. *Yom Ha-Esh* (*Inside the Miracle*). (Tr. by author.) Tel-Aviv: Karni, 1966.

Katznelson, Berl. *Ketavim* (*Works*). (Ed. S. Yavnieli.) 12 vols. Tel-Aviv: Ayanot, Mapai Publishing House, 1947–1955.

—— *Latent Values*. Tel-Aviv: Ayanot, 1954.

Kovetz Hashomer (*Hashomer Collection*). Tel-Aviv: Archion Ha-Avoda, 1937.

Lankin, Eliahu. *The Story of the Altalena*. Tel-Aviv: Hadar, 1967.

Lavon, P. *Values and Changes*. Tel-Aviv: Hamerkaz Letarbut Vehinuch, 1960.

Livne, Eliezer, *et al.* (eds.). *NILI toldoteyah shel he'azah medinit* (*NILI, The History of Political Daring*). Tel-Aviv: Schoken, 1961.

Min Hayesod. Tel-Aviv: Amikam, 1962.

Niv, David. *Battle for Freedom: The Irgun Zvai Leumi*. Vols. I and II, 1965; Vol. III, 1967. Tel-Aviv: Klausner Institute.

Peres, Shimon. *Ha-Shalav Haba* (*The Next Phase*). Tel-Aviv: Am Hasepher, 1965.

Ra'anan, Zvi (ed.). *Zava u-Mil hama B'Israel Uva'mim* (*Army and War in Israel and Among Nations*). Department of Guidance and Defence of Ha-Kibbutz ha-Artzi Hashomer Hatzair. Tel-Aviv: Sifriat Poalim, 1955.

Rosenstein, Zvi. *History of the Workers' Movement in Palestine*. Vol. I, 1956; Vols. II and III, 1966. Tel-Aviv: Am Oved.

Rupin, Arthur. *Pirkey Hayaye* (*Diaries*). Tel-Aviv: Am Oved, 1968 (Reprint).

Sadeh, Yitzhak. *Ma Hidesh Ha-Palmach* (*What Did the Palmach Innovate*). Merhavia: Sifriat Poalim, 1950.

Sepher Hashomer (*The Book of Hashomer*). Tel-Aviv: Davar, 1936.

Shamir, Shimon. *Toldot ha-'Aravim ba-mizrah hatikhon Ba-'et ha-hadasha* (*History of the Arabs in the Middle East in Modern Times*). Vol. I. Tel-Aviv: Sifriat Poalim, 1964.

Sharett, Moshe. *Yoman Medini* (*Political Diary*). Tel-Aviv: Am Oved, 1968.

Shayeb, Israel. *Ma'aser Rishon* (*First Tithe*). Tel-Aviv: 1950.

al-Tall, 'Abadallah. *Zikhronot 'Abdallah al-Tall* (*Memoirs of 'Abdallah al-Tall*). (Tr. Y. Halamish.) Tel-Aviv: Ma'arachot, 1960.

Tevet, Shabtay. *Massa' Zahal Be-Sinay* (*The Campaign of the Israel Defense Army in Sinai*). 1st and 2nd eds. Tel-Aviv: Am Hasepher, 1957.

Trumpeldor, Joseph. *Letters*. Tel-Aviv: Am Oved, 1946.

Tsur, Jacob. *An Ambassador's Diary in Paris 1953–1956*. Tel-Aviv: Am Oved, 1968.

Zabotinsky, Zeev. *Ketavim* (*Works*). 13 vols. Jerusalem: 1949.

ARTICLES IN FOREIGN LANGUAGES

Alami, Musa. "The Lesson of Palestine", *The Middle East Journal*. III (October 1949).

Allon, Yigal. "Israel at Bay", *Midstream*. II (Spring 1956).

Ben Gurion, David. "Israel's Security and her International Position before and after the Sinai Campaign", *Israel Government Year Book 5730.* 1959/1960).

Binder, Leonard. "The Middle East as a Subordinate International System", *World Politics.* X (April 1958).

Blair, W. Granger. "Dayan Quits Post in Israel's Cabinet", *New York Times.* (May 11, 1964).

Brice, Belmont. "The Military in Subsaharan Africa", *African Forum.* (Summer 1966).

Dayan, Moshe. "Israel's Border and Security Problems", *Foreign Affairs.* XXXIII, No. 2 (January 1955).

Deutsch, Karl W. "Social Mobilization and Political Development", *The American Political Science Review.* Vol. LV, No. 3 (September 1961).

Draper, Theodore. "Israel and World Politics", *Commentary* (August 1967).

Eisenstadt, S. N. "Israel", in Harold M. Rose (ed.), *The Institutions of Advanced Societies.* Minneapolis: University of Minnesota Press, 1958.

—— "Patterns of Leadership and Social Homogeneity in Israel", *International Social Science Bulletin.* Vol. 8 (Fall 1959).

Etzioni, Amitai. "Alternative Ways to Democracy: The Example of Israel", *Political Science Quarterly.* LXXIV (June 1959).

—— "The Israeli Army: The Human Factor", *Jewish Frontier.* XXVI November 1959).

Friedland, William H. "For a Sociological Concept of Charisma", *Social Forces.* No. 43 (October 1964).

Germani, Gino, and Kalman H. Silvert. "Politics, Social Structure and Military Intervention in Latin America", *Archives Européennes de Sociologie.* Vol. 2 (1961).

—— "Politics, Social Structure and Military Intervention in Latin America", in Wilson C. McWilliams (ed.), *Garrisons and Governments.* San Francisco: Chandler, 1967.

Guttman, Allen. "Political Ideals and the Military Elite", *The American Scholar.* Vol. 34, No. 2 (Spring 1965).

Halpern, Ben. "The Role of the Military in Israel", John J. Johnson (ed.), *The Role of the Military in Underdeveloped Countries.* Princeton: Princeton University Press, 1962.

Heymount, Irving. "The Israeli Nahal Program", *The Middle East Journal.* Vol. 21, No. 3 (Summer 1967).

Huntington, Samuel P. "Political Development and Political Decay", *World Politics.* XVII (April 1965).

Hurewitz, J. C. "The Role of the Military in Society and Government in Israel", in S. N. Fisher (ed.), *The Military in the Middle East.* Columbus: Ohio State University Press, 1963.

Janowitz, Morris. "Changing Patterns of Organizational Authority: the Military Establishment", *Administrative Science Quarterly.* Vol. 3 (March 1959).

—— "Military Elites and the Study of War", *Conflict Resolution.* Vol. 1 (1957).

Khadduri, M. "The Role of the Military in Middle Eastern Politics", *American Political Science Review.* Vol. 47 (1953).

Khouri, Fred J. "The Policy of Retaliation in Arab–Israeli Relations", *The Middle East Journal.* Vol. 20 (Autumn 1966).

Lerner, Daniel and Richard D. Robinson. "Swords and Ploughshares: The Turkish Army as a Modernizing Force", *World Politics.* Vol. 31 (October 1960).

Lewis, Barnard. "The Arab–Israeli War: The Consequences of Defeat", *Foreign Affairs.* Vol. 46, No. 2 (January 1968).

Lissak, Moshe. "Modernization and Role-Expansion of the Military in Developing Countries: A Comparative Analysis", *Comparative Studies in Society and History.* Vol. IX, No. 3 (April 1967).

—— "Patterns of Change in Ideology and Class Structure in Israel", *The Jewish Journal of Sociology.* Vol. VII, No. 1 (June 1965).

Moskos, Charles C. "Racial Integration in the Armed Forces", *American Journal of Sociology.* Vol. 72, No. 2 (September 1966).

Nasser, Gamal Abdel. "The Egyptian Revolution", *Foreign Affairs.* XXXIII, No. 2 (January 1955).

New York Times (December 28, 1964; June 5, 1965).

Nolte, Richard H. "American Policy in the Middle East", *Journal of International Affairs.* XIII (February 1959).

Perlmutter, Amos. "From Opposition to Rule: The Syrian Army and the Ba'th Party", *Western Political Quarterly* (forthcoming).

Perlmutter, Amos. "The Israeli Army in Politics: The Persistence of the Civilian Over the Military", *World Politics,* Vol. XX, No. 4, July 1968, pp. 606–43.

Pye, Lucian W. "Armies in the Process of Political Modernization", *Archives Européenes de Sociologie.* Vol. 2 (1961).

Rapoport, David. "A Comparative Theory of Military and Political Types", in Samuel P. Huntington (ed.), *Changing Patterns of Military Politics.* New York: The Free Press, 1962.

Rustow, Dankwart A. "The Army and the Founding of the Turkish Republic", *World Politics.* XI (October 1959).

—— "The Military in Middle Eastern Society and Politics", in S. N. Fisher (ed.), *The Military in the Middle East.* Columbus: Ohio State University Press, 1963.

Shils, E. A., and M. Janowitz. "Cohesion and Disintegration of the Wehrmacht in World War II", *Public Opinion Quarterly.* Vol. 12 (1948).

Smolansky, Oles. "Soviet Policy in the Arab East 1945–57", *Journal of International Affairs.* XIII (February 1959).

Weber, Max. "The Three Types of Legitimate Rule", *Berkeley Publications in Society and Institutions.* No. 4 (1958).

ARTICLES IN HEBREW

Allon, Yigal. "Active Defence—Guarantee for Our Existence", *Molad.* (April 1967).

L

—— "Deeds and Determination", in Zrubavel Gilad (ed.), *The Book of the Palmach*. 2 vols. Tel-Aviv: Ha-Kibbutz ha-Meuchad, 1955.

Amir, Yehudah. "Sons of Kibbutzim in Zahal", *Megamot*. Vol. 15, Nos. 2–3 (August 1967).

Antonovsky, A. "Socio-Political Attitudes in Israel", *Ammot*. Vol. 1, No. 6 (1963).

Bagrit, Leon. "The Modernization of Israel", *Ha-Boker* (April 4, 1965).

Bamachane (July 20, 1950; February 15, 1951; February 28, 1952; May 5, 1955; October 29, 1966).

Bashan, Raphael. "Interview with Allon", *Ma-Ariv* (April 12, 1968).

—— "Interview with Defence Minister Moshe Dayan", *Ma-Ariv* (June 9, 1967).

—— "Interview with Eban", *Ma-Ariv* (March 22, 1968).

—— "Interview with General Rabin", *Ma-Ariv* (June 13, 1967).

Bauer, Yehuda. "Riots or Revolt", *Ha-Aretz* (April 15, 1966).

Ben Gurion, David. "From the Diary: April–May 1948", *Ma-Ariv* (April 30, 1968).

—— *Hazon Va-Derech (Vision and Ways)*. "The Structure and Ways of Zahal". Vol. 1. Tel-Aviv: Mapai, 1951.

—— "On Dayan", *Ha-Aretz* (March 10, 1964).

Ben-David, J. "Professions and Social Structure in Israel", *Scripta Hierosolymitana*. Vol. III (1959).

"Camp Marcus", *Bamachane* (July 20, 1950).

Dayan, Moshe. "Relations with Arabs without Mediators", *Ha-Aretz* (June 24, 1966).

Dori, Ya'aqov. "Rebuttal on Ma-Ariv Symposium", *Ma-Ariv* (May 20, 1966).

Editors of *Bamachane*. "A Military Orientation in Zahal?" (February 28, 1952).

—— "Interview with Dayan" (March 10, 1967).

Editors of *Ma-Ariv*. "Interview with Generals Rabin and Yadin" (February 16, 1968).

—— "Interview with Prime Minister Levi Eshkol" (October 4, 1967).

—— "Symposium on the Sezon" (April 4, 10, 15, 24, 29, 1966).

—— "Symposium on Whether the War (1967) Brought Nearer the Peace" (February 16, 1968).

Eilat, Moshe. "Zahal Veterans toward the University", *The University* (Hebrew University Monthly). Vol. 12, No. 2 (July 1966).

Elitzur, Y. "Invaders to the Civilian Industries", *Ma-Ariv* (January 4, 1963).

Eshed, Hagi. "The Affair", *Ha-Aretz* (February 19, 1965).

Finkelstone, Y. "New Light on the Formation of the Jewish Legions", *Ma-Ariv* (May 14, 1967).

Galeeli, Israel. "The Palmach—A Seed of the Labor Movement", in Zvi Ra'anan (ed.), *Zava U-milhama (Army and War in Israel and Among Nations)*. Tel-Aviv: Sifriat Poalim, 1955.

Ha-Aretz. "On Lavon" (February 28, 1952; June–September 1955;

January 13, 1961; February 5, 1961; June 1960–April 1961; March 10, 1964; February 17–18, 1965; March 26, 1965; May 2, 1965)

Ha-Aretz Magazine. "Interview with Dayan" (January 19, 1968).

Haviv, Canaan. "How and Why was Yair (Stern) Assassinated", *Ha-Aretz* (February 24, 1967).

Hertzog, Chaim. "Industry and Security", *Ha-Aretz* (March 25, 1966).

Horowitz, Dan. "Between 'Pioneer Society' and As 'All the Nations'", *Molad* (October 18, 1960).

——. "The Permanent and the Transitory in Foreign Policy", *Min Hayesod.* Tel-Aviv: Amikam, 1962.

Katznelson, Berl. "Yirurim Al-Hamatzav Hakayam" ("Doubts on the Present State of Affairs"), *Ketavim.* Vol. III. Tel-Aviv: Mapai, 1949.

Lapid, Yoseph. "Is There a Danger that Zahal will Stage a Coup?" *Ma-Ariv.* (May 12, 1967).

Mor, Raphael. "The Alufim (Generals)", *Ha-Aretz Magazine* (May 5, 1967).

Nakdimon, S. "The Drama that Preceded the Formation of the National Unity Government", *Yediot Aharonot* (October 18, 20, 25, 27, 1967).

Offer, Philip. "Between the Army and the Civilians", *Ha-Aretz* (November 20, 1963).

Poles. "Ways Blocking an Alternative Government", *Ha-Aretz* (January 1, 1965).

Rosenfeld. "Interview with Dayan", *Ma-Ariv* (April 30, 1968).

Shamir, Ami. "Officers without Uniform", *La-Merhav* (January 20, 1967).

—— "Profession beyond the Military", *Bamachane* (February 1952).

Shiff, Zeev. "Controversies in the Defence System", *Ha-Aretz* (August 12, December 14, December 21, 1966).

—— "The Danger of Operational Entanglement in Zahal", *Ha-Aretz* (August 14, 1966).

—— "Lack of Balance between Zahal and the Ministry of Defence", *Ha-Aretz* (August 12, 1966).

—— "1936: Perception of Force toward the War of Independence", *Ha-Aretz* (April 15, 1966).

—— "The Qibya Raid", *Ha-Aretz Magazine* (December 10, 1965).

—— "The Third Round", *Ha-Aretz Magazine* (March 1967).

—— "The Three Weeks that Preceded the War", *Ha-Aretz* (October 4, 1967).

—— "The Young Officers of Zahal: Education and Political Consciousness', *Ha-Aretz* (September 18, 1963).

Shimoni, Ya'aqov. "The Arabs and the Approaching War with Israel", *Hamizrah Hehadash (The New East).* No. 47 (Jerusalem, 1962).

Tabenkin, Itzchak. "History of Ha-Kibbutz ha-Meuchad", *Mebefnim.* VII (July 1937).

Talmon-Garber, Y. "Differentiation in Collective Settlements", *Scripta Hierosolymitana.* Vol. 3 (1955).

Yadin, Yigael, *et al. Bamachane* (February 28, 1952).

—— "The War of Independence Interview", *Ma-Ariv* (May 14, 1967).

DOCUMENTS

"The Defence Ministry", *Israel Year Book 1950*. Government Printing House, Prime Minister Office (GPO/PMO), pp. 59–68.
—— Israel Year Book 1951. GPO/PMO, pp. 55–66.
—— Israel Year Book 1952. GPO/PMO, pp. 45–56.
—— Israel Year Book 1967. GPO/PMO, pp. 78–97.
Divrey Ha-Knesset (Parliamentary Debates). "Debate on Defence Service Bill", "Debate of Military Laws". Vol. II, No. 18–28, Meetings 50–80 (July 4–September 12, 1949).
—— "Debate on Lavon's Resignation". Vol. VIII (February 21, 1955).
Palestine Royal Commission Report. Summary. London: Her Majesty's Stationery Office (HMSO), July 1937.
Statistical Handbook Jewish Agency for Palestine, 1949.

NEWSPAPERS, MAGAZINES, AND PERIODICALS
(General)

Al-Ahram, daily (Cairo).
Al Hamishmar (Tel-Aviv), since 1948, organ of Mapam.
Davar (Tel-Aviv), 1925, daily of Histadrut, serves as mouthpiece for Mapai.
Ha-Aretz (Tel-Aviv), since 1918, independent daily, close to Progressive Party Left of Centre.
Ha-Boker (Tel-Aviv), 1936, General Zionist Party daily organ.
He-Homa, monthly of Haganah representing labour views, first published during World War II.
Ha-Mizrah he-Hadash (The New East), published in Hebrew with English summaries, quarterly of the Israel Oriental Society, vols. I–XIV, Jerusalem: 1949.
Hapoel Hatzair, weekly of Mapai, founded by Hapoel Hatzair party in 1906, labour's most distinguished magazine.
Herut, 1948–1965, daily of Freedom Party.
Hever Ha-Kvutzot, monthly of Hever Ha-Kvutzot from 1929 to 1950.
Ma-Ariv (Tel-Aviv), independent afternoon daily, 1948.
Mabat Hadash, Rafi's weekly, begun August 1965.
Mebefnim, monthly of Ha-Kibbutz ha-Meuchad since 1935.
Middle Eastern Studies, quarterly published by Frank Cass & Co. Ltd., London.
Min Ha-Yesod, Lavon's faction publication, begun in 1962.
New Outlook, monthly in English, vols. I–VII, Tel-Aviv: 1957–1964.
New York Times.
Niv Ha-Kvutzah, successor to *Hever Ha-Kvutzot*, monthly of Ichud Ha-Kvutzot Ve-Hakkibutzim.
The Palestine Post, English-language daily, since 1950, *Jerusalem Post*.
Palmach, monthly of Palmach, published between 1943 and 1949.
Ramparts.
Yediot Aharonot (Tel-Aviv), independent afternoon daily, 1939.

(Zahal's periodicals, journals, and magazines)

Bamachane (Zahal's weekly).
Bamachane Gadna (army youth weekly).
Bamachane Nahal (Nahal's weekly).
Ma'arachot (monthly).
Ma'arachot Yam (navy magazine).
Ma'arachot Himush (armoured magazine).
Bitaon Heil Ha-Avir (air force magazine).
Skira Hodshit (monthly review for Zahal's officers).

UNPUBLISHED MATERIALS

Arian, Alan. "Ideological Change in Israel: A Study of Legislators, Civil Servants, and University Students", unpub. diss. (Michigan State University, 1965).

Lissak, Moshe. "Social Mobility and Political Identity in the Israeli Society: Problems of Integration of Oriental Communities in the Social and Political Structure of Israel", unpub. MS. (Jerusalem: Department of Sociology, Hebrew University, May 1967.)

Perlmutter, Amos. "Arab Armies in Politics". (Berkeley: Institute of International Studies, University of California, 1966.) (mimeo.)

—— "Ideology and Organization: The Politics of Socialist Parties in Israel 1897–1957", unpub. diss. (Berkeley: University of California, 1957.)

—— "The Praetorian State and the Praetorian Army: Toward a Taxonomy of Civil–Military Relations in Developing Politics." (Berkeley: Institute of International Studies, University of California, 1967.) (mimeo.)

Rosenstein, Eliezer. "Social Change in the Israeli Society." (Berkeley: University of California, 1965.)

Weintraub, D., M. Lissak, and Y. Atzmon. "The Chequered Cloth." (New York: Cornell University Press, forthcoming 1968.)

Index

DATE DUE

1906